Arise Esther

Becoming Women Of the Kingdom

By: Angela Ramnath

BETHLEHEM PUBLISHERS

Arise Esther
by *Angela Ramnath*

Copyright © 2006 by Angela Ramnath

2nd edition 2010

Printed in India

ISBN 1-59781-906-9

All rights reserved solely by the author. The author guarantees all contents are original and do not infringe upon the legal rights of any other person or work. No part of this book may be reproduced in any form without the permission of the author. The views expressed in this book are not necessarily those of the publisher.

Unless otherwise indicated, Bible quotations are taken from the Student Bible NIV, copyright © 1986, 1992 by The Zondervan Corporation, and the Women of Faith Bible NIV, copyright © 1973, 1978, 1984 by International Bible Society.

www.bethlehempublishers.co.cc

Preface

Arise Esther-Becoming Women of the Kingdom is a refreshing approach to the life of Esther. It was truly edifying and inspiring to read this manuscript. The author took the life of Esther and made it practical for women in every area of society to pattern their lives after. It is truly a tool for women to mentor women. It also shows women that God created them for a purpose and with a purpose, and no matter what stage their life is at, if they begin to develop and apply the principles in this book to their lives, they can rise to the top and become an influence in their home, workplace, school, community, nation and the world. But, most of all God would give them the desires of their heart.

This book is a must read for all women who are preparing to become all that God created them to be, and those who desire a fresh encounter with the living God.

Ruth Munroe
*Co-Senior Pastor,
Bahamas Faith Ministries,
International.*

Table of Contents

Acknowledgements	v
Dedication	vii
Foreword	viii
Introduction	x

Chapters

1.	An Orphan	13
2.	A Woman of Purpose	17
3.	Pure at Heart	22
4.	Obedient	25
5.	A Woman of Faith	29
6.	Teachable	32
7.	Humble	36
8.	Submissive	39
9.	A Woman of Character and Integrity	44
10.	Beautiful	47
11.	A Positive Attitude	52
12.	Patient	57
13.	Compassionate	60
14.	A Woman of Passion	65
15.	A Woman of Influence	68
16.	Love and Intimacy	72
17.	A Worshiper	77
18.	A Woman of Favor	81
19.	A Warrior	87
20.	A Woman of Celebration	95

Acknowledgements

I want to give thanks to my Heavenly father and King for giving me this book that I have desired to write since the inception of the Esther Gathering Conferences in 2000. I thank God for His perfect timing. I sat down many times with pen and paper, but no words came to me, until June of 2005 when you started giving me these words. Words cannot express my gratefulness. Again, thank you Father.

I would like to thank the following people for your dedication and hard work towards this book. Without you, this project would have been impossible.

Thank you, Hannah Lackraj and Lilliana Ramjohn for turning my illegible scribbling into understandable English. This was one of the most difficult tasks, but you did it, and in such a short space of time.

Genesis and Mirlande Registre, thank you for taking time off from work to proof and edit the manuscript in such a timely manner. You knew I had a deadline, and you helped me to make it.

David and Rosanna Borman, thank you for not only editing, but for moving in with us for almost two weeks in the midst of hurricane Wilma and it's aftermath to help me to meet the deadline. Your determination to see this book completed still amazes me.

Siew and Sarah Radhay my parents, thank you for raising me with a certain standard that molded me into becoming the person I am today. I surely learnt the difference between right and wrong. You were great providers who made sure that my brothers and sister and I never lacked for anything. Your love and support even up to this day is unbelievable. I love and appreciate you.

To my spiritual parents Dr Myles and Ruth Munroe, thank you for introducing the Kingdom of God to me in such a profound way. My life has changed forever because of your teachings. Thank you for your love, prayers and support always.

To all my uncles and aunts who helped raise and mold me into becoming the niece that you are so proud, thank you for all the love and encouragement. You have a special place in my heart. My loving cousins, who support me and are always there for me, thank you so much for your love.

Anganee Pinto and Rhona Radhay my sisters, thank you for you tremendous support with this book, and especially for the song. My brother Anthony, thank you for the music. It means so much to me. God gave it to you because you are so dedicated and sold out to his Kingdom. May He give you many, many, more songs!

To the wonderful women at Miramar Christian Center International, thank you for being right there by my side. Your love and support is amazing. I always say that we are truly blessed to have all this beauty under one roof! Surely we are favored by God, and always know that you have a special place in my heart.

Dedication

I lovingly dedicate this book to the King of my life, my husband and friend, Pepe Ramnath. I fell in love with you from the very first time I saw you, and my love for you grows stronger every day. I look forward to us growing old together. What I like most about you is your encouragement in allowing me to be an individual person doing the things I like doing, and are called to do, without any barriers.

I also dedicate this book to our three children, Matthew, Joshua, and Leah. Thank you for you love and support you gave to me during this time of writing. You are three beautiful stars, true gifts of God. Thanks for being understanding and patient as Dad and I travel the world preaching the gospel of this kingdom; we could not do it without you. The three of you have a very special place in God. You are the best children anyone could ever have. Both dad and I are so proud of you. Continue to shine as children of the kingdom and serve Him forever.

Foreword

In every era of change a great leader always emerges that dares to be different. Esther was one of those great leaders. She was a woman of charisma, charm and great leadership. The book of Esther contains all the essentials and basic requirements for effective leadership to people who may have found themselves in very difficult places with cruel leaders like King Xerxes.

Esther prepared herself by seeking God's direction first. God almighty is the master mind of course, who knows the deepest secret of all men and women. This great woman of excellence consulted with God and received all the information she needed to convince a self centered King who had power to destroy her at the stroke of a pen or flick of a finger. Esther, however, was determined to make a difference in the lives of the people she loved so much that she was willing to risk her life for the cause that would change and shape history in favor of the Jewish people.

Jesus came preaching the Kingdom of God reconfirming the fact that the message of the Kingdom has been around since the creation of this world, Matthew 5:34. This was not a new message; it was here long before he began to preach it. This message of the kingdom was clearly demonstrated in the life of Queen Esther as she changed the earthly vicious kingdom of King Xerxes into a kingdom that was attractive and inviting to all people. She was definitely a woman of the Kingdom of God that the grounds she stood upon became territory of the Kingdom of God. The politics of the earthly Kingdom had to bow and change by her presence. She brought hope and courage to men and women from all walks of life by the way she dealt with the king. Her persistence and character will forever be a standard by which all of us could learn from. Esther's work was done with a rich history that will continue to live on and reshape the lives of great men and women that will dare to change this world with the techniques she used. The techniques of the Kingdom of God that Jesus preached.

This book, Arise Esther, Becoming women of the Kingdom, is written by an author that I have known personally most of my life. She is my wife of nineteen years of marriage and she had won my charms, by her much grace and strength as seen in the life of Esther. Angela has not only won my heart, and our children, Matthew, Joshua and Leah, but also, the hearts of the members of the Miramar Christian Center International in Miramar, Florida, and members of the body of Christ around the world. This book was written with great personal convictions that depict a passion for change through the skills and life experiences of the author as she remained steadfast on the teaching of Queen Esther. Her many challenging experiences have only helped her to become more like the Esther she wrote about in the following pages. And, without reservations, I highly recommend this reading and challenge you to read every chapter, for each chapter builds upon the previous. May you find the strength to become the woman of the Kingdom. See you at our next "Esther Gathering Conference" and may the God of Esther be with you as you find the pearl in the field of these pages.

R. Pepe Ramnath, PhD
Senior Pastor
Miramar Christian Center,
International

Introduction

As I read through the book of Esther, I thought, "Oh, what a story of courage and risk! Would I be willing to risk my life for people I do not know personally, who I am not even related to?" Esther was an inspirational leader, an incredible heroine and her story is *true*. Her legend lives on and should be studied and realized by every woman of this 21st century. Every woman, either young and inexperienced or older, can share their experiences through mentorship. Any woman, of any society can take example of Esther's heroic deeds and actions of well over two thousand years ago.

Yes, it's almost impossible to ever think that women of this day and age can relate personally to the struggles and triumphs Esther faced over two thousand years ago. However, if we do indeed strive to live an Esther like life, we will surely share together in her earthly triumphs and heavenly rewards. Some will cry, "But Esther was such a person of high moral and courage that her great sacrifices of that day would surely overwhelm us that we may feel we could never live like Esther!"

The Bible says that with God all things are possible to them that believe;

> *Jesus looked at them and said, "With man this impossible, but with God all things are possible."*
>
> Matthew 19:26

Esther was placed in the royal palace not by choice or coincidence but by the plan and purpose of God for such a time as this.

> *"For if you remain silent at this time, relief and deliverance for the Jews will arise from another place, but you and your father's family will perish. And who*

knows but that you have come to royal position for such a time as this?"

Esther 4:14

Therefore, women are placed in society in this millennium, for such a time as this. There are women all over the world suffering because they do not know their purpose for their lives, and are not living life to its fullest or becoming all they were meant to be. We were meant to be women of God's kingdom, we already have royal blood flowing and cascading through our veins, and all we need to do is change our mindset!

Chapter 1

An Orphan

Esther was the only person in her immediate family to survive the senseless hate crimes from the enemy at that time. From the beginning of time the Jews always had enemies trying to wipe out their generation because they were God's chosen ones.

Today anyone believing in Jesus Christ becomes Abraham's seed, heirs according to the promise (*Galatians 3:29)* and makes them a target of the enemy also. If you notice around the world Christians and Jews are hated more than any other group because of this.

Luckily or as I would say by faith, Esther had one kin who had survived the same fate, her cousin Mordecai. Thank God Mordecai was older than her and was established in the city of Susa in the Persian Empire. (Susa - an ancient city of the Babylonian, Persian and Parthian empires, situated about one-hundred and fifty miles east of the Tigris River, in the southeastern part of the modern day country of Iran.) Mordecai had a good job at the palace gates and a nice, cozy home in which Esther was raised. Esther made do with whatever Mordecai provided and never complained for anything except at times she would miss her parents terribly, and at those times God comforted her through her dear cousin Mordecai, as He always comforts His people in times of need.

He defends the causes of the fatherless and the widow and loves the alien giving him food and clothing.

Deuteronomy 10: 18

Mordecai was both mother and father to Esther, raising her up as his own child, and she grew up to become a beautiful, young lady in every way. How many orphans do we know of that are given the chance to grow up and become great people in our society today? Out of all the orphans I know, most of them had very difficult lives and grew up in bitterness and anger because they never let God heal them like Esther did.

My husband Pepe lost his mother at a very young age and his father some years ago. He recently told me that there used to be an emptiness and loneliness in his heart sometimes, but it never lasted too long because he says he has a wife at his side and his kids who fills the emptiness. He says that he finds a lot of happiness in me and I was very relieved to hear that! I am not that difficult to live with after all! He also has my parents whom he finds comfort in, along with his siblings. Now I noticed that his siblings, who were much younger than him and single struggled much more with the hurt and pain of losing their parents, than the married ones.

I do not know the full extent of the pain orphans go through. The closest I got to that is losing my little sister Annie. I was just about two and a half years old and she was one and a half. My mother told me that my sister and I were very close and we did everything together. I remember very vaguely some of the things that we did, however, I do remember the day of the funeral very clearly. Her little casket was placed on a table in my grandmother's living room, the place where we lived at that time. She had bluish discolorations from her accidental fall down the stairs. I dreamt her from that night on, and for about two years afterwards. Every night I would have the same dream that both of us were holding hands and running from one end of the yard to the next, and I would wake up gasping for air. I grieved a lot for my sister at that tender age.

Over the years I lost people very close to me like some of my uncles, aunts, cousins and grandparents. Those were very painful and difficult times for our family as well. Could you imagine what Esther went through losing both parents at the same time? It's hard to lose people you're so used to. It leaves a void. A void I know will be filled one day when we all meet again in heaven.

I saw in the news after hurricane Katrina hit Louisiana, Mississippi and Alabama in August 2005 that many, many people were crying, pleading and holding up pictures and names of their loved ones who were missing. They were separated during the hurricane and my prayer is that they will be united again one day soon. It was heartbreaking, and only God can comfort them if they will allow him.

Life is full of unpredictable events and the best way to cope is to pray for God's grace upon our lives and our family's lives daily.

Today God wants to know what traumatic past do you have?

What crisis are you going through at this time of your life?

What type of scars do you have inside?

Were you abused as a child or are you being abused now by a parent or a spouse?

Are you poor, unemployed, or on welfare?

Are you being treated like an unwanted stepchild, like Cinderella?

Are you an orphan, losing your parents through desertion, sickness or death?

If yes to any of these questions, you are qualified for God's attention, there is hope!

God says he will never leave you nor forsake you.

No one will be able to stand up against you all the days of your life. As I was with Moses, so I will be with you; I will never leave you nor forsake you.
Joshua 1:5

Though my father and mother forsake me, the Lord will receive me.
Psalm 27:10

As believers, becoming women of the kingdom, if we do not know the word of God, we will not be able to come out of the past and into this glorious kingdom that God has waiting for us. We will continue to live in the past that may have been filled with defeat and despair. But, if we continue or start a regular regimen of reading the word of God daily, we would come into the kingdom and all of its benefits much sooner. All you need to do is to get started. God is waiting to snatch you away from all of your past, and all of your pain and suffering and bring you into His royal courts, the place where you belonged all this time!

Chapter 2

A Woman of Purpose

Approximately between 460-350 B.C., Jerusalem was destroyed by King Nebuchadnezzar of the mighty Babylonian Empire, and the Jews were held captive there. Sixty years after these events, Babylon was then conquered by the Persian Empire. The captive Jews were set free and were allowed to return to their lands. Some of the Jews adapted to the Persian culture and decided they did not want to go back to Israel. Many Jews remained and made their permanent home in Susa the Persian capital.

Esther happened to be living in Susa at that time. She was of royal origin for she was from the bloodline of King Saul from the tribe of Benjamin, a descendant of King David. She had royal blood flowing through her veins, but as a teenager growing up in such a simple setting, she did not realize how noble she was. Esther was not placed in that simple setting by chance, for there was a reason. It was all God's doing. According to the Persians, Mordecai and Esther and all the other Jews had no status in their Persian society. Although the Hebrew law did not regulate adoption it was allowed because of the Bible verse:

Do not take advantage of a widow or an orphan.
Exodus 2:22

God cares for the disadvantaged and will take care of them.

When God needs someone to do something in the kingdom, I believe He already knows and has it in His mind who to use, when to use them, and where to find them. He knows His children of purpose, the ones who will say yes to the call no matter how difficult the call would be down the road. All God wants to hear is, "Yes Lord, I will do your will, whatever you want to use me for," and the induction begins. When you are chosen by God to do something, know that He has already favored you and given you the grace to do the job. It does not matter what background you came from. The only pre-qualification you need is a ready and willing heart.

When Mary was chosen by God to fulfill her purpose, the mighty angel, Gabriel appeared to Mary and said:

"Greetings, you are highly favored and the Lord is with you, you have found favor with God and you will have a son!"

Luke 1:28

How many of us could answer immediately without doubting or denying something like this?

Mary remained calm, and replied;

"I am the Lord's servant may it be unto me as you have said!"

Luke 1:38

She spoke, knowing that she had no choice in the matter because it was a command from God. She also knew that God would have simply selected another holy virgin to take her place. She was pleased to respond to her purpose, the thing she was born to do. Then Mary sang with joy.

"My soul glorifies the Lord and my spirit rejoices in God my Savior for he has been mindful of the humble state of his servant.

Luke 1:47-48

In real life, who would rejoice and sing after finding out that they are pregnant and unwed? It's only when you know that it is God's will for your life, that you can say yes without saying, "Not me Lord, I cannot do this, did you know I cannot sing, I cannot preach, I cannot dance, I can't, I can't, I can't!" But if we are like Mary and we know God's purpose for our lives we will not need any persuading, but will submit at once.

Mary was willing to risk everything to fulfill God's will for her life. Her engagement and future marriage to Joseph, her reputation with everyone in her community for having a child out of wedlock, and ultimately, her life was at risk.

The reason for Esther living in Susa at that time was for a much higher purpose than just survival. God had great big plans for her life. Never question why God placed you in the country you were born. He has great plans for you. When Esther was taken into the palace against her will to compete for Queen of Persia, she did not try to run away, or commit suicide. She did not know all that was ahead of her, and that not retaliating, but cooperating with the authorities would make her queen, or that she would be responsible for the salvation of an entire nation. She had no idea of what risks and hard work lay ahead of her, but she knew it was God's will and decided not to fight it.

An example of this would be what happened shortly after hurricane Wilma hit South Florida in October 2005. I saw in the news that some people were very upset and stated angrily how much they hate Florida and that they are leaving the state. Only people who do not know their purpose would let such petty things as climate and fear drive them away from their place of destiny and purpose.

As women of the kingdom, when we are called upon to do something, our purpose that we were born to do, we need to make haste and do it or else God will choose another. He doesn't waste time to hear the excuses why we can't do it. When King Xerxes summoned his first wife, Queen Vashti to appear before him, she refused fearing his drunken state. When Queen Vashti refused to be displayed in front of the king and his guests, she was exiled at once, never to have any royal privileges again. When Esther was called, she walked into the palace regardless of how frightened or how unsure she was, just like a chosen person would do. She went through the entire journey until she saw her great victory.

As a Pastor's wife I see good examples of this. Some

people come to the church, see their purpose and are ready to work immediately in the area of their gifting. They are so excited; they can't wait to become members to get started in their area of calling. I feel so happy to know that total strangers can come into our church and feel like family, and make themselves right at home, because the truth is, they are not strangers but family of the Body of Christ. Those people get to work at once. Then there are others who come in and we have to spend time with them and study with them to help them discover what their purpose is in the church. Most of the time, they do not even know what their gifting is, and when we do see the potential in them, we have to pull it out with a bulldozer. It may take years to do this in some cases.

It's very sad when people do not know their purpose. Dr. Myles Munroe said in his book, In Pursuit of Purpose, "Fulfilling purpose must be the primary goal of every person and without purpose life is an experiment or a haphazard journey that results in frustration, disappointment and failure, and time has no meaning." He further states that, "All things begin and end with a purpose, that purpose is the destination that prompts the journey."

I was thinking; even laboratory rats have a purpose. They are used in experimental procedures to test the safety of food and medication before they can be administered to human beings. They are also used in the study of different disease development and tolerance compared to humans. God predestined us with a much higher purpose than that of a lab rat. We were not created to be an experiment but as a time traveler, fulfilling the purpose given to us as we pass through this earth, performing the experiments and procedures of this journey of life. Therefore, we are the experimenter, not the experimented.

We were created by God not by chance, but for a great purpose. We are so very valuable in the sight of God, much more than any other creation. Pepe says that human beings are walking millionaires! The human body is made up of all the finest chemicals and minerals, including gold, silver, copper and many more. If all these precious compounds were added up, the total would be way over a million dollars! We are worth more than we can ever imagine.

The next time you feel discouraged or poor, all you need to do is to look in the mirror and remember your great value and worth. Know that you were created for greatness and there are no exceptions. If you already know your purpose, get started with your assignment. It brings a feeling of satisfaction to walk in purpose. Our primary calling is to tell the good news of Jesus to the lost. I always feel most complete and satisfied after witnessing and leading people to God. There is no greater joy. You do not have to be an evangelist to be a witness to the lost and searching people. It's the basic calling of every believer.

If you do not know your purpose, get started with your quest to find it, and don't stop until you find out what it is. Ask your pastor to help you. There is a spiritual gift test that our new members take to determine where they belong, and it really helps in placing them in the area of their calling.

Do you know what your purpose is? If the answer is yes, then start walking in it. It's only when you find your purpose, you can really start living!

Chapter 3

Pure at Heart

I believe that the first qualification of being chosen by God is having a pure heart. There was this great assignment and vacancy for one of God's agents to be placed in the Sushan palace, and this vacancy was needed to be fulfilled by a Godly woman, who sought after God's heart, one of God's most qualified agents.

Esther was brought in by God to fulfill this assignment. She did not pray for God to give her all the money in the world. She was a simple and satisfied woman only after one thing, and that was God's will for her life. God needed someone who was used to fasting regularly. Someone who was used to missing a meal or two, so that when the time came in the future to fast for three days and nights, they would not be too uncomfortable with it.

He needed someone who was broken so that He could easily remake them and their resume to fit the plan, His masterpiece. This is a request by God Himself:

"This is the one I esteem: he who is humble and contrite in spirit and trembles at my word."

Isaiah 66:2

Esther fit that description perfectly. She was surely broken, poor, and had nothing to lose. Most importantly she was not materialistic, nor vain.

Is someone on your job or in your life holding the position you should have had? Well, it's not for too long. God has a way of bringing justice to His children and when He says it's your time for promotion, no one can come against you, even if they try, because you have God's promotion, protection and blessings. If God is for you, who can be against you? This justice was surely experienced by Esther.

I believe Esther was blessed like the sermon at the beatitudes :

Blessed are the poor in spirit, for theirs is the kingdom of heaven. Blessed are those who mourn, for they shall be comforted. Blessed are the meek, for they will inherit the earth. Blessed are those that hunger and thirst for righteousness, for they will be filled. Blessed are the merciful, for they will be shown mercy. Blessed are the pure in heart, for they will see God. Blessed are the peacemakers, for they will be called sons of God. Blessed are those who are persecuted because of righteousness, for theirs is the kingdom of heaven. Blessed are you when people insult you, persecute you and falsely say all kinds of evil against you because of me. Rejoice and be glad, because great is your reward in heaven, for in the same way they persecuted the prophets who were before you.

Matthew 5:3-12

Esther was blessed because she was pure in spirit, she mourned, was meek, she hungered and thirsted after righteousness, she was merciful, pure at heart, a peace maker, persecuted for righteousness and falsely accused.

If any of these things relate to you, then you are qualified to be blessed. Rejoice and be exceedingly glad for great is your reward in heaven. If you are not sure that you are qualified to be pure at heart and blessed, it's easy to remedy. The Bible tells us to examine ourselves and return to the Lord if we stray. Please read the scripture *Lamentations 3:40*.

Once we examine ourselves, we ask God's forgiveness and repent. We denounce all things that make our hearts impure, and strive never to do them again. Once we embark on the journey to become a woman of the kingdom, our lifestyle has to change. We will have to stop going to certain places, eating certain foods and dressing immodestly. Our speech will have to change to that of a queen. The immoral movies and soap operas we watch will have to be done away with. A spiritual and physical house cleaning has to take place. All lustful pleasures must be given up. Our immoral friends will have to be changed towards connecting with people who could encourage and motivate us towards things of the kingdom.

Our new lifestyle should include: Daily prayer, praise and worship, repentance and reading of God's Word. Do not worry about losing friends and becoming lonely because of your new lifestyle. God will send the right people into your life as you draw closer to him. He wants you to seek Him first.

"But seek first the kingdom and his righteousness, and all these things will be given to you as well."
                                                            Matthew 6:33

Strive to be pure at heart and God will use you like he used Esther.

Chapter 4
Obedient

But Samuel replied: "Does the Lord delight in burnt offerings and sacrifices as much as in obeying the voice of the Lord? To obey is better than sacrifice, and to heed is better than fat of rams."

1 Samuel 15:22

Esther was obedient first to God and then to her cousin Mordecai, who raised her. There were no reports of her rebelling in any way against him. She was not disobedient or rude to him. In previous conversations with Mordecai concerning her future and marriage she left it up to Mordecai to decide on a spouse for her. She made it clear to him that she will accept whomever he would choose because she knew that he had good judgment.

Even at the time of her capture, she obeyed Mordecai when he told her not to reveal her identity or her real name, Hadassah. Also she did not run away and try to escape from the palace. I am sure around that time she was remembering the story of Joseph and his capture and confinement in the Egyptian Palace. However, he survived and later on became Governor of all of Egypt because of his obedience and commitment to God.

I believe Esther was cool, calm and collected as she remembered the Word of God to the prophet Jeremiah as he was suffering in exile:

"Before I formed you in the womb I knew you, before you were born I set you apart; I appointed

you as a prophet to the nations."

Jeremiah 1:5

Then the Lord reached out his hand and touched my mouth and said to me, "Now I have put my words in your mouth. See, today I appoint you over all nations and kingdoms to uproot and tear down, to destroy and overthrow, to build and to plan."

Jeremiah 1:9-10

She must have also remembered the scripture;

"For I know the plans I have for you," declares the Lord, "plans to prosper you and not to harm you, plans to give you hope and a future."

Jeremiah 29:11

  Her only hope to survive this ordeal was to remember and repeat God's word in her mind and let His will be done. Was it a coincidence that Queen Vashti was exiled just because she disobeyed the king, and did not appear when he called for her to come so that he could show her off naked before all his guests? Queen Vashti must have been sick and tired of the 180 days of feasting and partying. She might have just taken some headache medicine and went straight to bed, not wanting to be disturbed by a bunch of drunken men. The king and his royal subjects could not stand the thought of the queen disobeying the king, so she was exiled, banished for life, never to be seen or heard of again.

  Can you imagine a man not only divorcing, but also exiling his wife for not obeying him? In this 21st Century everyone would have been divorced and exiled if that law was still in effect! Women would have been put away on a separate island, no, maybe a continent just for being disobedient wives! Thank God for His mercy and grace upon our lives today.

  As a child growing up, I remember clearly there was a price to pay for any disobedience to my parents, neighbors, relatives and teachers. In my time, anyone who found me doing something wrong, who had the authority to scold me, would give me the rod of correction or tell my parents of my wrong doings. I never escaped the discipline wherever I went! I thank God for it today because it helped me turn out to be a better person. I thank God for my father's discipline. He did not allow me to go to certain places or associate with certain people. I did not understand back then all the reasons why he was adamant about those rules, but now that I am a parent, I clearly understand his logic of discipline!

We are now living in a different age. An alarmingly high rate of kids today does whatever they want and usually get away with it. Discipline is not like it used to be and that's why there are so many problems in this world, with so many broken families. There are so many teens in prison, it's heartbreaking. Just as the discipline of prayer was removed from public schools, the rights to being rebellious and lawless moved in. It's now a risk getting on a school bus or entering a public school. Prayer for students and teachers has to be increased more than ever before.

As kingdom women we need to know the King's decrees and commandments for our lives and obey them. The reason the Ten Commandments are being removed from public places is because Satan wants a lawless, rebellious and disobedient world of people, people he can easily manipulate and work through to do his evil deeds. It may seem difficult to obey every one of the commandments and not break any of them, but through Christ all things are possible. Once we have the Word of God buried in our hearts it will be easy to obey.

Here's a little motivation for obeying God's commandments the next time we feel a little white lie, gossip, murder, fornication, or adultery coming on. Read and study the following Scriptures;

If you fully obey the Lord God and carefully follow all his commandments, the Lord God will set you high above all the nations on earth; you will be blessed in the city and blessed in the country. The fruit of your womb will be blessed and the crops of your land and the young of your live stock, the calves of your herds and lambs of your flocks. Your blanket and kneading trough will be blessed, you will be blessed in your coming in, and your going out.

Your enemies who rise up against you will be defeated before you. They will come at you in one direction but will flee from you in seven. Your barns and everything you put your hands to will be blessed. God will bless you in the land he is giving you. God will establish you as a holy people and all people of the earth will see that you are called by his name and they will fear you. God will grant you abundant prosperity and open the heavens, the storehouse of his bounty to send rain on your land. You will lend too many nations, but you will borrow from none.

You will be the head and not the tail; you will always be at the top, never at the bottom.

Deuteronomy 28:1-13

These scripture are then followed by curses for not obeying God's commands. I believe that Esther chose to obey rather than to disobey and watch what God was about to do in her life.

Chapter 5

A Woman of Faith

Esther was a woman of great faith and that was the number one reason she became queen of the entire Persian Empire. Being a Jew was an asset that most of the other virgins did not have since they were Persians who believed only in idolatry and paganism. But Esther knew the real God Jehovah, the God who parted the Red Sea for Moses and the Israelites as they were fleeing Egypt. We know this is true because it is found in *Exodus 14:21.* Her God also caused fire to appear on a green tree and yet the tree did not burn, the God who caused the earthquake to take place so that the Jordan River could be dammed for twenty one hours so that Joshua and the Israelites could cross over to safety.(*Joshua 3:16.*).

He was the God who wrote the Ten Commandments with his own fingers onto the tablets, found in *Exodus 20.*

Esther remembered the story of Ruth how she went from being a poor, gentile, widow and foreigner, having to go through the humiliation of gleaning in the fields in order to eat. She later became the wife of the owner of the fields, a millionaire named Boaz. Not only did this poor, gentile, foreigner marry this rich man Boaz, but she was highly favored by God that she was blessed with a son called Obed. Obed then had a son named Jesse. Jesse then had a son who ascended to the throne of Israel, King David. This being the lineage from which Esther was born, and then continued for centuries afterwards when Jesus was born!

As lonely and depressing as the palace seemed, Esther

made the best of it. She knew that God was about to do something great in her life and just trusted that He knew what's best for her.

What are we believing God for in our lives? The bible says that all we need to have is faith like a mustard seed. I was thinking, a mustard seed is a small but very powerful seed. We need to believe with all our hearts that God can do it for us. We develop faith by hearing the Word of God as stated in *Romans 10:7*. The more we go to church and listen to the sermons, the more our faith is developed.

I remember in the late 1980's when we lived in New York City, I had a terrible urinary tract infection with all the painful symptoms. I still insisted on going to church that day ignoring Pepe's pleas to stay home and rest. I just knew I must be in the presence of God that day. I could not miss a day of not dancing and praising my God, and hearing His wonderful words. So, I hopped on the train and went off to church with Pepe.

That particular Sunday, the pastor was preaching on *Galatians 3:29* how the blessings of Abraham are upon us gentiles because we belong to Christ and we are Abraham's offspring, the rightful heirs according to his promise. It was the first time I ever heard that scripture in my life. I said, "Wow! That means me too!" I almost jumped out of my seat with joy! But I couldn't, because the pastor would have had me ushered outside! Suddenly, the pain from my infection stopped at once. When I got home there were no signs or symptoms of my infection. I was completely healed just by hearing the Word of God! The infection that usually reoccurs in 99% of people never came back again!

All God wants us to do is to please Him by believing His word. He said in *Hebrews 11:6 that without faith it is impossible to please God*. God is not pleased when we worry and cry. He said that all things are possible to them that believe.

Esther proved that the poor can be rich and strong, and the condemned can be set free just by being a woman of faith. Try having some faith like Esther had, and see great miracles take place in your very life today. If God did it for Esther he can surely do it for you.

Chapter 6
Teachable

As leader over our Esther Gathering Women's Ministry at Miramar Christian Center International, I am blessed with the best bunch of women anywhere in the world. Sometimes I am so thankful to God that I say He handpicked this bunch of beautiful women just for Himself and me! They make my life so much easier. How could it be possible to have all this greatness under one roof? There is no fighting, gossiping or bickering. All I get is lots of love and cooperation. I must say that these women are very teachable. I guess it could stem from the fact that Pepe is always advising me to teach the women to become like Esther, changing the hearts of the kings (husbands) in their lives, so that there would be better marital relationships. I guess he wanted to benefit too, if I am like Esther, then his life would be better also!

As women, we need to strive to become more like Esther, changing the hearts of our kings without having to say a word. Whew! What an awesome assignment! But, if Esther could do it, we can too. We just have to become *teachable* like Esther was. When Esther and the other virgins were brought into the harem, they were told that they would be going through an intensive transformation for twelve months through daily treatments that would prepare them emotionally and physically to go before the king. Esther had to start from scratch. She was raised by Mordecai, a man who most likely had no expertise in fashion, poise, speech, etiquette or posture. However, he did teach her all the other things where God, morals and decency was concerned.

Esther had no resume, no higher education and no premarital counseling. Many women in this 21st Century have great resumes, higher education and premarital counseling and still end up in bad relationships and divorce. What's the difference? It's simple, Esther was teachable. She was willing to change her life around to please the king. It was all about the king and his needs. She was not selfish and was definitely not only concerned about her own feelings. All she knew was that she had one visit that one night, one chance to impress the king and it was all that mattered. She quickly had a mindset change, "I am going to learn all that I can from those eunuchs, and they know the king's heart better than I do." Eunuchs were castrated men who were chosen to work in the harem on behalf of the king, taking care of, and training the virgin candidates. They were castrated to avoid any temptation from seeing the beautiful virgins day after day.

After the initial audition, she was told she needed a year's worth of training! She had to learn to walk, talk, dine, dress, look, smell and act like royalty in one year. She had to learn to say thee, thou and thy without biting her tongue! She had to learn to walk as if she had a book on her head, or appear as if she was walking on water! Yes, that could take a year or even more for me too!

Esther found the courage within herself to begin her journey of transformation. She probably kept repeating this scripture in her mind all the time:

The Lord is my strength and shield.

Psalm 28:7

She knew that although she was unqualified, she had a king who was higher and more qualified than King Xerxes, who had all the expertise she would ever need, her great God, Jehovah.

Esther became so teachable that she left it up to the eunuchs to tell her what to wear since she knew that they knew the king better than her. She did not pretend to know it all like some of the other virgins.

Do you fit Esther's background? No education, no resume, no experience or no upper social status? Then you qualify to become like Esther, a woman of the kingdom. Just remember, the sooner you get started with the lesson, the sooner you will graduate. And do not quit in the middle of the lesson, or else you will have to start the entire lesson over every time you quit.

Find a mentor who can teach you from their experiences and sit at their feet and learn all you can. Mentors are necessary in the development of leadership and character. They are the ones who transfer wisdom and teach discipline. A mentor is never your "buddy" who tells you only what you desperately want to hear, but what you *need* to hear. Their words may not always be soft, but words that may cut to the bone. A mentor is a person who you have great regards for, full of experience and expertise in the areas of your calling. They may be male or female, and should either be nearby, or easily accessible.

Mentorship requires investment of your time. A good protégé invests their time in the presence of their mentor and away from crowds. Since Pepe and I have found good mentors, it accelerated our lives in the areas of solid leadership and productivity. For instance, Mordecai was Esther's mentor. She submitted herself to him, allowing him to fashion her profound characteristics that she would use later on in life to please the king. Esther confided all of her fears to Mordecai that led to the defeat of Haman and his hateful strategies against the Jews. You can just as well apply your mentor's teachings to conquer your enemies.

Let me ask you this question today. Who provides your spiritual guidance?

Who speaks into your life and points you in the direction you need to go in life and ministry?

Who is protecting you from your ignorance and fears?

Who is *your* mentor and who are *you* mentoring?

Women of the kingdom should strive to have good mentors

in their lives, and become mentors as well, for this is our calling. Many young women today are in desperate need of mentorship. Get started today. The king has all the resources and He is waiting for you.

Chapter 7
Humble

Humility was one of Esther's unique traits. We may think that humility is a simple thing and that it's easy to be humble, but it's not. It's a characteristic that's not found in everyone. Have you noticed, a person who is not humble is usually arrogant and self-centered and gets nowhere in life? King David, one of the most humble men in his time said;

> *"Who am I, O Lord God? And what is my family that you have brought me this far? You have looked on me as though I were the most exalted of men."*
>
> 1 Chronicles 17:16-17

Even though God did not want the temple to be built by David, David did not take offense that God would choose another to do this great task. David prayed and repented more than anyone else in the bible, and that's what kept him humble. *Micah 6:8* says that God requires us to act justly and to love mercy and to walk humbly with him.

Jesus revealed the importance of humility in the following scriptures :

> *At that time the disciples came to Jesus and asked, "Who is the greatest in the kingdom of heaven?" He called the little child and had him stand among them. And he said: "I tell you the truth, unless you change and become like little children, you will not enter the kingdom of heaven. Therefore, whoever humbles himself like this child is the greatest in the*

> *kingdom of heaven. And whoever welcomes a little child like this in my name welcomes me."*
>
> Matthew 18:1-4

God wants us to come before Him, not pretending to have all the knowledge or know all the answers, but as women who will sit at His feet like children hungry to learn what He has to teach us. People who never went through any heartaches, trials or poverty usually do not understand what it is to be humble. That is the reason why Jesus was born in a manger. It shows that no matter where we come from, we can become great in life, like Jesus was. Humble beginnings are the stepping stones to our successes later on in life.

When the young, rich man asked Jesus what he must do to inherit eternal life, Jesus told him to sell everything he had and give it to the poor, that he may have his treasure in heaven, and then follow him. The man grew sad, and then went away. This true story is found in *Matthew 19:16-22*. That man had great wealth and could not part with it *even* for the sake of his soul and salvation. Then Jesus said;

> *"Again I tell you it is easier for a camel to go through the eye of a needle, than for a rich man to enter the kingdom of God."*
>
> Matthew 10:24

This happens because most of the time rich people in the world have everything they need and do not see the need for God in their lives. They fail to think about the future and their destiny. In *Matthew 5:5* Jesus tells us *"Blessed are the meek for they shall inherit the Earth."*

Esther was an orphan, not an heiress to a kingdom at the time she was chosen. She humbly came into the kingdom with only the clothes she was wearing, but because of her humility, she would later inherit a whole kingdom. To be humble is to be yourself. Do not act or pretend to be somebody you're not. Have you ever seen some friends who act like twins? They talk the same way, dress the same way, copy each other in every way and then you're lost thinking who is copying who? God made us unique women. We all have our own personalities, ethnic backgrounds, accents and looks. Please do not lose these original features that we were constructed and designed with. We must have the mindset to *first* please God and God alone, then everything else will fall into place.

Be humble and God will exalt you in due time, for this is His request. God said in *Matthew 23:12 whoever exalts himself will be humbled, and whoever humbles himself will be exalted.* Wouldn't it be a shame if you had to be humbled by God? It may not look nice; it may be just as ugly as how Haman's life ended up. When we are exalted or honored by God, it's a great thing and everyone will rejoice with us, as with Esther's case.

Chapter 8
Submissive

I believe the "S" word as we fondly call it, is the most difficult requirement of women. This curse of the pain while childbearing and the desire to rule over our husband started in the Garden of Eden. God cursed Eve, and that curse will be transferred down to every woman after her, forever.

> *To the woman he said, "I will greatly increase your pains in childbearing: with pain you will give birth to children. Your desire will be for your husband and he will rule over you."*
>
> *Genesis 3:16*

Many Bible scholars believe that this verse means that Eve will naturally want to rule over her husband, but he will rule over her! I say, because Eve got Adam to do her dirty deeds once, why wouldn't he do it a second time? Some men seem to be so easily convinced, and some men don't even need any convincing to do everything their wives tell them to do even if it's wrong in the sight of God! If Esther submitted despite the curse, women of the 21st Century should be able to submit also because we believe in the same God as Esther did.

Webster's dictionary defines submission as a means to show honor and devotion to.

> *The bible explains the reason why we should submit. Wives submit to your husbands as to the Lord. For the husband is the head of the wife as Christ is the head of the church, His body, of which He is the savior. Now as the church submits to Christ, so*

> *also wives should submit to their husbands in everything.*
>
> Ephesians 5:22-24

Your husband is the high priest of your home, the king of the castle.

Certain cultures teach this custom of reverence to husbands in a very extreme fashion, mostly in the Eastern and Asian world. When I was living in Trinidad, a western country, because of tradition of our great grandparents who came from India, women were taught to treat their husbands like gods. They were to spiritually and physically worship their husband treating them much higher than themselves. This included bowing down and touching their feet as a sign of respect. You would see a man walking down the street, his wife behind him with the kids. You would observe that the man would not lift a finger in the house. The most those men would do is go to work outside the home, but once they come home it's the wife's turn to serve him.

I've seen some women take off their husband's shoes and socks, bring the food to them on the table or couch, then take the empty dishes away and bring water to wash their hands right there where they are seated. I have seen when the men were ready to take their bath, the wife has to run and get their towel and clean clothes. I've known of women being cheated on and not able to say a word to their husbands about it. Some were physically or mentally abused with no place to go to. I thank God that I was saved before I got married, and I also thank God for sending me a great husband so that my life could be different than those women from those other cultures I had witnessed growing up.

When we were married in 1986 I was an independent woman. I had a good job, which was one of my goals that I finished college before I got married, and I did. I was a registered nurse making decent money. I had my own car, friends and church activities that kept me busy. I was actively involved in my church, especially in the youth department.

Just before our first wedding anniversary, we moved to New York City where Pepe had lived since 1981, going to college. I felt like God removed everything from my life that made me comfortable. I was away from my family, friends, car, job, youth department and church. I had no one there except for Pepe and a very few of his family members. I was also pregnant at the time. I had to start from scratch all over again by trying to find a job and a decent apartment. Thank God for Pepe's aunt Dolly who let us live in her one bedroom apartment for three months while we were getting settled. Pepe was already living with her for five years before I got there, and I don't know how she survived all this!

I went from being a registered nurse to a kitchen helper while I was studying to do the nursing state board exams, which I had to repeat a few times. It was not until after a year and a half later that I started to work as a nurse again. I believe that God had to completely strip me of everything and have me start all over again so that I could learn to depend on him as my source, not my self-made career, and, also to have me make less money than Pepe so that I could see him as the head of my home and submit to him. If I had money and friends I may not have submitted, and probably would not have even been married for all these years! God had to remove me from everything. I guess that's what it takes in some people depending upon our level of submission!

Pepe had to show me around, teach me the modes of transportation: trains, buses, and sometimes the luxury of a taxi, when I was in labor! I had to go from zero submission and learn fast because it was not easy. There were many, many fights and disagreements on the way that would take another book that I will write later on to tell you of all the adventures of being newlyweds in New York City! I am proud to say today that my submission level is way up now, I would say maybe 99%. Nobody is perfect. I hope Pepe will agree!

With these lessons I went through earlier in my marriage,

I am more likely to submit now than ever before. I also realize that at times if I do not submit there are always consequences and a price to pay. I tell Pepe it's easy for me to submit to him now because I'm convinced that he loves me and he will *not* take advantage of my submission. Back then as a newlywed, I was insecure and did not know how much he loved me, but as time went by I became more aware of his love for me and all my insecurities faded. My submission is now to the point where if he says don't spend money foolishly, only buy what I absolutely need, then I submit. I will only buy the basic necessities: food, clothing and diamonds!

    I believe that Queen Vashti did not submit because she had everything and never had to suffer for anything, so she did not see the need for submission. Esther on the other hand was broken, grew up around simplicity with nothing to lose. Yet, she had to submit to a king she did not know much about. She did not even know if she would like him, let alone love him, but she submitted because she trusted that God was with her and he would not put her in a position where she would be hurt or destroyed.

    When the slightest things happen to us we ask, "Why me Lord? What did I do to deserve such punishment? " God loves us so much and wants the best for us that He would set us up to go through certain rough times just to bring out the best in us. If we learn to submit to Him and our husbands, we can avoid many of these painful lessons. We may not understand all that God is doing in our lives at this time but know that it's all for our own good.

All we need to do is trust God:

Trust in the Lord with all our heart and lean not on our own understanding; but in all our ways, acknowledge him, and he will make your paths straight.

Proverbs 3:5

Remember that if God started a work in you, do not try to figure out how He will do it, but know that He will complete it as He promised and did for Esther.

Chapter 9
A Woman of Character and Integrity

A wife of Noble character is her husband's crown but a disgruntled wife is like decay in his bones
Proverbs 12:4
If you walk before me in integrity of heart and uprightness as David your father did and do all my commands and observe my decrees and Laws I will establish your royal throne over Israel forever.
1 Kings 9:4-5

Esther's story made it in the Bible because of her character and integrity. She was established upon the royal throne and became a legend, heroine of Israelites because she followed the king's decrees and laws. She did not go into the palace saying, "I do not like things the way they are, and I'm going to change it." Whatever was the palace's requirement for her, that's what she adhered to.

Proverbs 11:22 tells us that a woman with all the great looks, glowing skin, beautiful curves, shiny healthy hair, but no character is like a pig wearing a shiny gold ring in its nose/snout. To say this, God is really concerned about our behavior, more than our looks. A beautiful woman is not only what she looks like on the outside, but it's what's on the inside as well. How she thinks and acts is what matters. God has a perfect example for us to follow when He describes the *Proverbs 31* woman. Sounds impossible? I used to think so until I learned that with God all things are possible. It means that women can have theses high standards just like the virtuous woman.

Esther remained a virgin until she got to the king. She did not say I have no parents to be accountable to so I could live how I want to, and go wherever I want to, and sleep with whomever I want to. She had no professional counseling for her childhood traumas and yet did not grow up to be an angry, rough or mean person. She was not ill tempered, loud or rude. If she was, she would not have been liked by anyone including Mordecai. He would have been happy to see her taken away from him.

In her marriage to the king, Esther knew when to keep her peace and when to speak. When she had to tell the king about Haman's wicked plans to wipe out the Jews, she did not immediately run into the throne room and blurt out to the king in front of all his eunuchs about it. When she heard about the plans, she remained cool, calm and collected. Realizing that the king had to be in a certain mood to hear these things she designed a strategy in which to do it. She was wise to discern the king.

Women should also be wise to discern the kings in our lives. When we go to God we need to discern if it's time to ask Him for stuff or if it's time to praise Him, or bow down before Him and cry out. When it comes to our husband, we need to know that when he comes home from work, that we do not immediately tell him all the bad things that happened to us today. Most men detest this and we need to be wise and discerning as to when and where we break certain news to them.

I have noticed when Pepe comes home after a long, hard day's work he needs to wind down for at least an hour before engaging in any serious conversation. When he gets home in the evening, he sits in his favorite recliner. I bring him a drink, then dinner on a tray, give him the remote control and let him switch channels for at least an hour! Then I put away the remote and it's my time! We then talk about issues. Pepe always says how badly he feels about me serving him like that and spoiling him, but I assure him that I do it because I want to do it and not because I have to.

We do not have to tell everything all at once, most things can wait. Esther was patient no matter how urgent the matter was. She was so confident that God would move on her behalf at the right time. How can we develop character and integrity? It's easy. We need to follow the pattern placed before us in *Proverbs 31*. If we develop great character we will be looked upon by our husband and children as worth far more than rubies, and blessed above all women. We should strive to be good to them always. Be nice, use soft words of love and encouragement. It is also very important that we keep our word. If we say we are going to do something, then we need to do it because I have heard too many disappointing stories from unbelievers about Christians not doing what they say they would do. We are looked upon to uphold a certain standard as believers, although we are mocked and scorned at the same time. The world is still looking for perfection from us. Let us be that light that will ultimately guide those who are searching for an answer, towards the Kingdom of God.

We need to work. Whether at home or outside in the workforce, we should always keep busy. If we are blessed to be stay at home moms, which is even more difficult than working outside, we should spend our time making the home beautiful, not sleeping or on the phone all day or looking at soap operas. We should be so very busy doing more important things with our precious time like cleaning, cooking healthy meals, making ourselves beautiful, praying, studying and learning more of God's word. Sounds like a too perfect life? Well that's God's request for us. He said in *2 Corinthians 13:11: aim for perfection.*

Colossians 1:28 says *it is possible to present everyone perfect in Christ. And remember, all things are possible to those who believe.*

Chapter 10
Beautiful

It is said that Esther was one of the four most beautiful women in the Bible. Her name in Persian language means "star" or "radiating with beauty." The other three women were Sarah, Rebecca and Rachel. Although Esther had all that beauty in her, she still was not fit to appear before the king's presence. She had to go through the preparation process just like everyone else, from the inside out. First, the purification and detoxification process that would last about six months, then the beautification process with perfumes and cosmetics. This would last another six months.

This process was described as follows: first half of time rubbing myrrh and ritual cleansings. This included herbal deep cleansing, laxatives, changes in diet, plucking of eyebrows and hair in armpits, legs, etc. by waxing or threading. This really hurts. I tried using a do it at home waxing of the legs and upper lip one day. I had a scar on my upper lip for at least a week since I accidentally removed a lot of skin! And, I was to accompany Pepe on a speaking trip in the country of St. Thomas the Virgin Islands. I knew that everyone was staring at me wondering what happened! What a first impression. And, my leg waxing, if my daughter Leah was not home that day to help me peel the adhesive tape full of wax off my legs, I would have surely died of pain!

The first six months for Esther was not easy. It's not easy being a beautiful queen. The other six months included painting of hands and feet with henna, milk baths, infusions of incense to the hair and skin, application of mixtures of paste to lighten the skin, and removing blemishes, and make up to face.

One day while Pepe and I were out of town, I took a do it your self facial mask. It seems like I'm always trying do it your self merchandise because I do not always have time to go to the spas. While Pepe was taking a nap in the hotel room, I decided to work on my face. I put a facial mask on and lay down next to him. I had to wait for the 15 minutes to go by to peel it off. Pepe woke up soon after and said, "Oh..., what happened?" He was scared that my face had turned gray and rough. I had to assure him that it was only a beauty treatment and that it was removable. Sometimes during the beautifying process we do not look that great, but we need to keep on doing it because the results will make both you and your king happy. Humans were the only creation who was blessed with the technology to create and use make up, not the angels or any other animals. Let's make good use of it.

The women at MCCI love to try new things. One day a group of us decided to treat ourselves to the spa. It was an experience to remember and I wish we could go back at least twice a year. This did not happen yet! This was our experience; first stage, we were placed in a dark, quiet room on little massage bunk beds. Our feet were massaged and reflexology performed, and this was my favorite part, since my insteps always seem to hurt from those high heels. We were then taken into the bathtubs which were filled with water and relaxing mineral salts.

We each had assigned to us the masseuse and while we're soaking in the tub they massage our scalp, neck, shoulders and back, rubbing away all the stresses of life. (Another favorite of mine) Then we were taken out of the tub and placed in the steam room. It was so steamy in there that you could barely breathe, and then you get used to it. The steam allows toxins to be released through the skin by sweating profusely. This was a near death experience, not my favorite. After surviving the steam room we earned three to five minutes in the water fall. We sit on a bench and water falls on our back massaging and cooling us off from the steam room. This is also very relaxing.

Once we are cooled off, it was time to go into the sauna. This is almost as hot at hell as I have imagined. Charcoals are burning on a furnace that gives out more heat than the steam room. You feel you're literally being slowly smoked like a ham with the charcoal flavor. The heat further removes toxins. I had to close my eyes most of the time in this one to prevent them from melting, really!

After this it's break time. We were served a light lunch, spring salad with a few chunks of goat cheese and two croutons, and iced tea. After lunch the fun starts again, the dreaded facial, most painful. A bright light was shining directly on my face so that I could not see a thing. The blackheads and whiteheads are squeezed out from places I never knew had them. My face was also steamed by a steaming machine to open up the pores before the removal of the blackheads. My face was blotchy, red and slightly swollen for the rest of the day from the trauma.

Next it was time for the manicure and pedicure. Cuticles were cut and pushed back; feet were sanded down to remove dead skin. Both hands and feet were then dipped in hot wax and wrapped in plastic bags for about 10 to 15 minutes. This is called the paraffin treatment. After this we can shower, change and go to the last phase, the hair. Even though you say you just washed your hair upstairs, it's not good enough for the beauticians. They believe that no one can wash hair like them, so they rewash the hair. Then the final phase was to blow dry and style. This was where your head is moved in every direction possible, wherever the hair brush will carry it!

After this, the day at the spa had come to an end. We are ready to face the world to let everyone see what a day at the spa did for us, ready to go home to our kings who were waiting patiently. Would anyone like to go with us next time? This was just one day at the spa. Imagine Esther had to go through this every day for almost one year.

If we want to be beautiful like Esther was, no matter how beautiful we think we are, we have to go through the preparation and purification process. We cannot go to the king covering our blemishes, faults and ugliness. Make up alone will not do it. We have to start from the inside out. Purge our inside with spiritual laxatives and repeat, to get rid of ugly ways.

Proverbs 30:30 tells us that *charm is deceptive and beauty is vain, but a woman who fears the Lord is to be praised!*

Beauty goes far beyond physical appearance. If we want to be beautiful we must be beautiful not only in looks alone, but by our ways, the fruits that we display. My daughter Leah told me one day, "Mom, you are the prettiest old lady I know!" I never thought that the day would come when the words pretty and old would be used together in the same sentence to describe me! Oh, how I need another spa treatment, maybe cosmetic surgery right away!

Leah also asked me one day when was I born. When I told her the sixties, she said, "And you're still alive!" I had to assure her that people born in the sixties are now only in our forties and we have no plans of dying any time soon!

In preparation for the king we need to also prepare ourselves spiritually. Before our Esther Gathering conferences we go through vigorous preparation. Even before the hair and nails etc, the women department teams up with the intercessory department to fast and pray for three months prior to the conference. We fast and meet weekly for prayer and then the last three days, we do the Esther fast which is no food, but water only. We prepare like this because our desire is to see lives changed forever, hearts are healed, freed and mended as the Esther anointing falls on them. We have seen great results from these conferences because of the preparation, and this is taken back to the homes, churches and communities of everyone attending.

Why do we prepare like this? It's because the Lord

commands us to.

Amos 4:12 prepare to meet your God.

We should not go to Him without preparation. We purify because *we are God's people, eager to do what it good* as explained in *Titus 2:14*. When we finally approach our God, we would be beautiful both inside and out and we will be in right standing with Him and worthy of His glory upon our lives all because we strived to be like Esther!

Chapter 11
A Positive Attitude

I believe that if Esther did not have a positive attitude, she would have tried to run away from the palace or commit suicide when she was first taken into captivity. Imagine the culture shock, taken away from her Jewish home and suddenly placed in a palace with a pagan king, a place of no Godliness. She had to eat foods that were against her religion and dress according to the Persian fashions.

She was being prepared to go before a king who was probably twice her age and very powerful. This empire that he reigned over stretched from India to Ethiopia. He was a dangerously impulsive king and any province he could conquer was his. The only reason he did not acquire Greece was because their army was too strong for him. He had built his palace in the middle of his empire, in Susa.

At one time when a bridge he had ordered to be built was destroyed in a storm, he commanded that the sea receive three hundred lashes, and then had the bridge builders beheaded.

I am reminded of some world leaders today who were that strong and impulsive. People like Adolph Hitler who hated the Jews and tried to wipe them off the face of the Earth, just as Haman was doing in Esther's time to annihilate all the Jews in the Persian Empire. In the 1970's the wicked leader Idi Amin, Prime Minister of the African country of Uganda sent out death squads to murder all those who opposed him. Christians, the British and Asian society, mainly of Indian descent were told to leave the country. He told them that God told him to have them expelled. In the 1980's Sadam Hussein's government repressed movements that it deemed threatening, particularly those from ethnic or religious groups. He had thousands killed and tortured during his evil reign. He believed in capital punishment and made sure that everyone saw that he did not tolerate crime or opposition, by holding public executions.

Imagine Esther being prepared for the king who was not as evil as these men, but yet, overly ambitious for wealth and power. A man who exiled his former wife Queen Vashti because of disobedience!

As Esther was soaking in the mineral salt bath one day she over heard some of the other young ladies talking about another incident. One day one of the king's loyal subjects contributed a large sum of money towards a military expedition. The king was so enraptured that he returned the money along with a handsome gift of his own. But when the same man asked the king to let just one of his sons go free from the army's draft, King Xerxes became so outraged that he ordered that man's son to be cut into two pieces and have the army march between the pieces. That's the king Esther was to sleep with and possibly marry.

Esther, being the strong willed person she was, knew that she could not go before the king with her attitude or her life could be in danger. She had to change her entire mindset and do it quickly. She had to become even more humble than she thought she was. She was at the king's mercy and there was nothing she could do, time was approaching fast. There was no chance of meeting and getting to know the man she would marry as she thought would happen one day in her life.

There would be no dating for two years, and no premarital counseling. Her religion and culture condemned all that she was about face, to sleep with a man before marriage, a man who was not a Jew, a man who slept with so many other women before her, a risk of sexually transmitted diseases and pregnancy. She had to keep the secret and not reveal to anyone that she was a Jew.

Who in their right minds, facing all these circumstances, all at once would display such a great, positive attitude that even the eunuchs was so moved that they moved Esther up in line in front of some of the other virgins?

Only Esther had on the mind of Christ, the fruit of the spirit, the long suffering that would take her through. She was content in every situation like *Philippians 4:12* tells us. Knowing that God gives the strength to endure, Esther was enthusiastic and optimistic because she knew God would never let her suffer for any reason. When you are chosen by God to do something, no matter what comes you way, even if you want to scream and run away, you can't.

God gives a peace that surpasses all understanding, a love that casts away all fear.

1 John 4:18 explains that *perfect love casts away all fear.*

As we are becoming women of the kingdom, we need to examine ourselves. We cannot go into the king's presence with any stinky attitudes. If Esther who had such a great attitude still had to change and tone down, who are we?

Sermons are continuously preached about Christians who do not display a Christ like attitude. Pepe had an experience to remember as he attended a great, big miracle crusade one day. When the pastor called for all the other pastors to go forward for prayer, there was a big stampede. Everyone ran forward. They did not care that they were not pastors; their aim was to push themselves past the pastors and get to the front of the line! He had to brace himself from getting physically crushed. The saints of God are not always too saintly!

Non-believers have described Christians in the work place as being spooky and weird, and that they would be hexed by these Christians. That's because they display a spirit of religion and no fruit of the spirit. When they get angry on the job they threaten and speak in tongues! I've never seen this type of behavior save any one. It scares people away. At MCCI, people with that type of attitude cannot stay around. Pepe and I do not tolerate it. We confront and eradicate these super religious people because most of the time they are set in their ways and will not change.

Women of the kingdom are called out and chosen to do great things for God. We have to start our process of change. Make up may hide blemishes and discoloration but it cannot hide what's inside: anger, ill temperedness, hatred, bitterness and frowns. Change starts from deep within us. We need to examine our selves like King David did constantly in *Psalms,* and repent daily.

Psalms 19:12: who can discern his errors? Forgive my hidden faults.

People do not usually see their faults in this day because of self righteousness.

If you O Lord kept a record of sins, O Lord who could stand?

Psalms 130:3

We are all sinful before God. Let's admit this and we will be on our way to great things.

As we examine ourselves, we need to consult with the Holy Spirit to see what the King likes or dislikes. We can also consult our pastors, elders, leaders and spouses. The one closest to us would be the best ones to help us out. Ask them what they are seeing in us that may not be pleasing to God and unpleasant to other people. I know if I ask Pepe he will not hesitate to point them out to me! Most times I do not even have to ask him, he is constantly trying to help me improve, it's not always nice, the truth hurts sometimes, but then it brings about change that is critically needed. I do the same with him, and so, we help each other out. Time is going by fast and we do not have time to waste these days. We need to change fast. Esther had almost a year to change. Let's take the challenge and try to be different in a year's time. Get a friend who is willing to do it with you and help each other through. Let's see what we will be like in a year from now.

My daughter Leah asked me one day if she had and attitude. I looked at her sweet little face and I could tell that she as hoping for a yes. So I said yes you do have an attitude, but just a little one. She said, "Oh good, I got it from you!" I had to smile. I could not deny it. She is used to hearing all the time what a great kid she is and how she took her father's genes, his looks and ways etc, so I guess she wanted to have something from me!

The Lord's word is all the motivation I need for me to change even more rapidly.

Your attitude should be the same as that of Jesus Christ. Who being in very nature God did not consider equality with God something to be grasped, but made himself nothing, taking the very nature of a servant being made in human likeness. And being found in appearance as a man, he humbled himself, and became obedient to death, even death on a cross!

Philippians 2:5-8.

If we put on this attitude of Christ then we will be like Jesus, unstoppable! Satan tried to stop Jesus early in his ministry during the initial forty days fast by offering him bread and water. Satan tried again during the crucifixion by telling Jesus if he was indeed the son of God, he should save himself. Jesus could have stopped his death, but he knew that conquering death was what he needed in order to go into hell and take the keys from Satan, defeating him forever. So pick up the attitude of Christ, like Esther did. This attitude will give you many victories.

Chapter 12

Patient

He gives strength to the weary and increases the power of the weak. Even youth grow tired and weary and young men stumble and fall, but those who wait upon the Lord will renew their strength. They will mount up with wings like eagles, they will run and not grow weary, and they will walk and not faint.

Isaiah 40:29-31

This must have been Esther's daily scripture quotation as she got up from bed very early in the morning to start her daily routine. It was good that it was almost one year and not one week before her date with the king or else she would have gone insanc. She had to be prepared physically, emotionally and spiritually for this and the more time to do this the better.

I am sure some of the young ladies in the harem could not wait for their turn to go before the king regardless if they were ready or not. But, Esther was going to be patient regardless of how frustrating it seemed, sometimes tripping as she was learning to walk properly, leaving at the end of the class thinking she would never be able to act like royalty. Thank God that Hegai saw potential in Esther and believed in her even if she could not believe in herself. She had to continually remind herself that she was born with a purpose for such a time as this, that God is doing something great in her life even when she could not see it. She knew that all things worked together for good for those who love God. So she rest assured that there would be a great ending to all this drama some day.

She was waiting patiently, taking it one day at a time until one day Hegai pulled her aside and said, "Esther I have done something for you. Because you have shown such patience and strength and have been the best student here, I'm going to move you up, even while the other girls laughed at your mistakes, the other eunuchs and I have been watching you closely. You did not lose your temperance or curse out at anyone. Your patience is far beyond anything we have seen, and we decided that you are ready to go before the king tonight. You are the perfect candidate for King Xerxes, we think he will like you a lot, even fall in love with you and make you queen!"

In the middle of going through certain situations, if we are patient and wait upon the Lord, He promises to renew our strength. Yes it's tough at times but ask God for grace to go through the lessons because God can show up in the middle of it and say; "it's your time to come before me daughter," like it happened to Esther.

When Esther's turn came to go before the king, she asked for nothing except what Hegai suggested.
Esther 2:15

Esther's time had come and so will your time come, just hold on a little while longer. Esther did not choose a dress, shoe or jewelry. She left it all up to Hegai since he knew what the king would like better than she did. All she had to do was put on the right mindset. As she was getting dressed with fine clothes, makeup and jewelry, she was also putting on Romans 14:17 Righteousness, Peace and joy.

All her fears subsided. She felt a great peace that she could not explain. Despite the words and looks she got from the other girls, she could not see them or hear them. Her eyes were blinded from their hatred and jealousy. She felt nothing but joy. She was walking in the perfect plan of God and nothing or no one else mattered but the king, herself and her God. No one could stop her destiny now. She was off to the king's chamber where her life could be changed forever. Esther went through all the training, teachings and attitude adjusting to build a foundation for a great big project as we will see later on.

The Empire State Building in New York City in its construction had to go down about four stories into the earth before it could have gone up over 100 stories into the sky. It is said that the higher one goes up the deeper the foundation.

How deep is your foundation?

Is your foundation still being built?

Does it seem like you've been going down, down, down, for too long?

Just know that God is building a foundation in you, and then he will put you in the escalator and elevate you up, up, up to the top above your enemies. Your circumstances will only be stepping stones, and you will look down at them one day and thank God for them. Be assured to know that whatever work God started in you, he will be faithful to complete it. We know this to be true as this is said in Philippians 1:6.

Chapter 13

Compassionate

When Esther was told about Haman's plot to wipe out the Jews, her own people, she was moved with compassion and she was going to do something about it at once regardless of the danger she would be in. When you are called by God to do something, he will give you whatever it takes to carry out that mission. In this case Esther needed compassion, and she had so much of it that she would be uneasy until her task was completed.

It reminds me of Mother Teresa who was so full of compassion that she devoted her entire life helping poor, sick and dying people in India. She will always be my greatest human hero and I know I will see her someday in heaven. She said that we will never know how much good just a simple smile can do for someone, much less the acts of charity and kindness.

I believe that she was so full of love that it made her compassion easy. She spoke a lot about love. She once said, "Give of your hands to some and your hearts to love." If we are full of love then we will have no problem having compassion for others. As we continue to put on the mind of Christ we will become more compassionate as Jesus was. Jesus was not ashamed of His compassion either. In John 11:35 Jesus wept when He saw Lazarus sisters mourning when Lazarus died. He felt the pain that they felt, and had to do something about it. So despite Lazarus being dead and buried for four days, Jesus was going to defy death and bring Lazarus back to life again, regardless of how rotten the situation was.

When Joseph saw his brothers come to Egypt during the

famine, he went aside and wept. Since he was promoted to Governor of Egypt he could have put them to death or in prison for what they mercilessly did to him all those years back. But he was moved with compassion and treated them well instead. He also remembered the dreams he had about the wheat trees bowing down to him (his brothers), so he knew that it had to come to pass.

I remembered when I was a little kid, there used to be a few well known beggars in our town going from house to house at least every week begging for food etc. My mother, who was very compassionate, would pack groceries including rice, flour, and sugar or whatever they said they needed and send them away very happy. Pepe said that his mother did the same thing with the beggars because she was also a very compassionate person. He only lived seven houses away from us in the same little town. Now, both Pepe and I do the same thing as our mothers did back then. We have that same compassion like our mothers to give to the poor and needy and we find people wherever we go who are in need.

We pray to God for more money all the time so we can bless the needy in a bigger way than we do already. We thank God for blessing us with the gift of compassion that Jesus, Esther and Joseph had. I believe it's because of that compassion we have no lack in our lives.

I had an aunt who reminds me very much of Mother Teresa. Her name was Vio. She lived in a very small two bedroom house made of wood with dirt floors near a beach in Trinidad. She had five children and I would be the sixth child during weekends, summer, spring and Christmas breaks. Despite her limited space, she and her dear husband, always made room for those less fortunate than themselves, taking in homeless boys and girls who had no place to go. She delivered all the babies born in that little area, most of her neighbors and their children, and also her grandkids, expecting and usually receiving nothing in return. I do not know of any professional training she had in this area of expertise. She did not even finish elementary school but she was as gifted as any nurse I ever saw. Her story is an example that shows if you follow your purpose God has set for you He will give you the required expertise to accomplish your purpose.

As a child, my aunt was always in and out of the hospital for asthma and other problems, including a bad knee. She developed so much compassion that she refused to let her own health problems get in the way of helping all the other patients in the ward, because her love for the sick and needy was too strong. Satan uses poor health in believers to try and stop them from fulfilling their purpose for the Lord. Fight sickness by faith and take care of your physical body by prayer and eating the right foods. And try reaching out to others despite your own condition.

One time Aunt Vio took in a very ill young lady who had sores all over her body. Her husband and family refused to take care of her because of the stench and sight of the sores. My dear Aunt took her in immediately and nursed her for over a year until the young lady died in peace. Aunt Vio would have been a great help to Mother Teresa. Another time a man, who had crawling maggots in both of his legs, heard of her workings and compassion. He went to her for help since he was not getting better at the hospital. My aunt worked with him every other day until he was healed completely. She was not afraid of exposing herself to the diseases of the sick because she trusted in God that He would keep safe. She had no medical supplies like latex glov or surgical masks. The lab coat she wore for protection was the Word of God.

When people are hurting they need to see faces around them that care. This friend of mine told me about her experience at the emergency room recently when she was sick. It was horrible. She said she met the most uncaring workers, especially the clerical people who took all the information and paperwork. It amazes me that people with such attitudes, like pigs, are allowed to work in places like that where people are already sick and need the most caring people around them. I always say that everyone who works in public places must, and should take mandatory classes in ethics and etiquette.

This is needed even in the church today because people bring their attitudes into the church also. They think that being tough and mean is a good thing. I had to do an etiquette class in nursing school, and I am so thankful to God for it because it helped me so much, especially now that I am in the public so much representing God. As women of the kingdom we need to be discerning and observant. We need to see those faces that are sad and in pain, those that are grieving and suffering, those that are poor and needy, and become compassionate towards them. Speak a soft word of encouragement to them, do a good deed depending on the need.

Mother Teresa said, "Have you ever experienced the joy of giving? I don't want people donating just to get rid of something; I don't want you to give me what you have left over; I want you to give from your want until you really feel it. Sometimes our mission department asks for clothing to send away to different countries in need. Our missionary has to say all the time, "Please do not bring clothes that are stained or have holes, but bring something that you can still wear." It's sad when we have to tell people this over and over. Jesus said:

> *As often as you did it for the least of my brothers, you did it for me.*
>
> *Matthew 25:40*

When we give to the poor and needy we give to God, when we have compassion for others we have it for God, and God will be pleased with us. Let's give our best because we are giving it to God, so give it with love.

> *If I speak in the tongues of men and of angels but have not love I am only a clanging cymbal, If I have the gift of prophecy, faith to move mountains but not love I am nothing, If I give all I possess to the poor surrender my body to the flames, but have not love, I am nothing. Love is patient, love is kind, does not envy, does not boast, is not proud, is not rude or self-seeking, is not easily angered, keeps no records of wrongs. Love never fails. And now these three remain: faith, hope and love, but the greatest of these is love.*
>
> *1 Corinthians 13*

Chapter 14
A Woman of Passion

One of my previous Esther Gathering conference themes was becoming women of passion. I believe that passion is a characteristic that women of today should acquire, if we do not already possess it. The movie, The Passion of the Christ by Mel Gibson, was a great example for us. It clearly indicated the reason for Jesus being on the Earth and the strong enthusiasm and determination he had to see that His purpose was carried through even unto death. Only passion would have made him go through with it. Therefore, I believe that passion is a gift given by God. What kept Esther happy even during her capture and detention in the harem?

It was passion.

Daniel was saved in the lion's den because of his passion. Shadrach, Meshack and Abednego were saved from the fiery furnace because of their passion. Joseph survived betrayal by his own flesh and blood and imprisonment in Egypt because of his passion. Jacob was willing to work for fourteen years just to marry the love of his life, Rachel, because of passion. If we have a dream great enough to change this world, God will give us the passion that it takes to do it.

Although passion is a God given gift, some people can misunderstand it and use it negatively. They use it for their own gain in the form of strong emotions, manipulation, anger outbursts, and lust for sex and wealth. We hear of stories of people going all out of the way to gain riches, stepping on everyone around them to do it. I have seen good businessmen and women throw their families aside for more money and it only led to destruction later on. Yes, it's good to become rich, but what are we planning to do with the riches, hoard it in a bank, or help those less fortunate than us?

Passionate people are willing to take risks. Esther said that she was going to go to the king on behalf of the people, and whatever the king chooses to do to her, so be it. She didn't mind losing her own life for the cause. Dr. Martin Luther King and Mahatma Gandhi died fighting for the rights of their people. They did not live to see it but the cause of their protest did eventually pay off. Abraham Lincoln would have probably lived a longer life if he had not proclaimed freedom to the slaves in the early 1860s but he chose to do the right thing. William Tyndale would not have been burned to the stake in 1536, if he had not translated the Bible into the understandable English language. Look at how this risk affects us believers today. We would not have been able to understand the precious promises that God has in His holy word for us.

I believe that Esther's passion grew as she approached the king that day un-summoned, and that passion caused the king to hold out the scepter towards her. I think that this gesture of the king was very romantic. Then he offered her up to half the kingdom and she refused it. She did not care about the riches as much as she cared for King Xerxes.

Who would ever have a party and invite their worst enemy? It would only be a person who is not afraid of the enemy, a person who has passion. Have you ever done something daring in the name of God? Sometimes God tells me to do something and I cry at first because pride is in the way, and I am scared of being rejected, but I do it anyway. It's passion that helps me to obey God, without it I could not do anything. When you have passion you will find yourself doing a lot of things by yourself because no one will ever want to accompany you. Sometimes I have to do many things alone, like sky diving and bungee jumping!

When I think about passion, I think about the disciples who

followed Jesus, even after His death. They split up and single-handedly traveled by foot all over the world after Jesus left the earth, spreading the good news to everyone. And, that's the reason we are all saved today, because of their passion that Christ transferred on them. Jesus said that the harvest is ready but the laborers are few. Can we sign up with him to be laborers? We have enough work to keep us busy for the rest of our lives here on earth. There should not be a day in our lives that we should say that we are bored. We are all placed here to dominate the earth. If we are to dominate, we need to get busy and start the process. Rocker Rod Stewart sang a song titled, "Passion" some time ago. He sang, "I need passion, you need passion, somebody somewhere needs passion, even the President need passion." The truth is we all need passion.

Women of the kingdom, let's walk in passion. If you think you do not have enough passion, it's easy to acquire. Just ask God to put some of His passion in your heart and He will.

Chapter 15

A Woman of Influence

Influence is action invisibly exercised. It's having people around you to do the things just like you do, without you saying a word to them about doing those things. It's like fashion. Someone wears the latest styles, and without anyone actually telling others to wear it, they go out and find those styles. We have seen many cases of influence over peoples' lives around us, some good and some bad. Even back in the bible days we look at the power of influence and its consequences.

First, Eve in Genesis 3, after being influenced by the serpent, in turn influenced her husband. Adam ended up eating the fruit that contained the knowledge of good and evil. The consequences still continue up to this present time. Because of this influential act, humanity is fighting to survive morally and spiritually today. We are all born in sin and shaped in iniquity. Thank God Jesus showed up to show us the true way to get out of this curse.

Sarah had much influence over her husband Abraham in Genesis 16:2 to carry out God's will for their lives, or so she thought. She caused him to have a child with their servant Hagar, and those consequences are still affecting the world today by the constant tension between the Israelites and the Arab world. Even the Christians are innocently terrorized today because of this.

Jezebel had much influence over her husband King Ahab. In 1 Kings 19 she caused a great king to fall under her evil powers and be influenced to the point of the murder of hundreds of innocent prophets of God. He had become the most wicked king that Israel ever saw.

Delilah's influence over Samson in Judges 16 shows us that the strongest, most powerful, Godly men could be influenced by an alluring woman, if he exercises no self control.

We can find numerous stories of influential women in the Bible, and also, in our world today. We find as women, that we possess these characteristics of being able to influence both in good and negative ways. Stories of great influential women in the Bible are those like Esther who influenced the king and saved a nation. Ruth was a great influence over her mother in law and Boaz in the town of Moab, and became a millionaire. Debra was the first female judge, and was also a prophetess of Israel. She was well respected as a woman of honor and courage that when she sent for a man Barak to lead the army, he was unwilling to go into battle without her. She predicted that the real hero of the battle would be a woman. Please refer to Judges 4:19.

There are also women of great influence in our world today. I will not dwell on the ones that brought negative influences, but rather, the ones who had great influence. In 1979, Mother Teresa won the Noble Peace Prize for her undying love and service towards the poor sick and dying people in Calcutta India. Due to her great humility, she had to be convinced to accept the prize. She gave the money (one million dollars) towards the poorest of the poor.

Florence Nightingale, a great woman who had such compassion for wounded British soldiers, began to nurse them back to health. She then sought for compassionate volunteers to help her. It later brought about the birth of the nursing field that's a critical part in people's health and recovery today. I am glad to be a part of this nursing organization today.

Since Mrs. Lori Mosley became Mayor of Miramar in 1999, she has done wonders in our great city. The city has undergone so much new construction of roads, new city hall building (nothing I have seen in any other city) traffic lights, housing developments, parks and community centers. I have never seen a city progressed in beauty and development like the motto says, so quickly. I hope she can remain Mayor as long as the law permits her for the great job she has done and is still doing. She has surely been placed here in Miramar for such a time as this. She also hosts some of the greatest parties in our city! She is a great influence to us women in Miramar and we love her dearly.

As we become women of the kingdom, we will definitely become women of influence. We need to channel this influence properly and positively, by the influence of love.

By this evidence everyone will know that you are my disciple, if you have love for one another.
John 13-35

When I think about love, I think about Jesus, my family and friends, family in the church, Mahatma Gandhi, Dr. Martin Luther King, Abraham Lincoln and all the influential women I previously named, people who would not mind giving up themselves for others. Love consumes selfishness. You can tell people's relationships for God by their love for one another and how they treat other people.

C.S. Lewis said, "To love at all is to be venerable. Love anything and your heart will certainly be weary and possibly broken. If you want to be sure of keeping it intact, you must give your heart to no one." He also said, "The only place outside of heaven where you can be saved from all the dangers of love is hell."

As women and mothers, we are in constant observation by our spouses, children, friends, neighbors and co-workers. We influence lives every day. Unsaved spouses can be influenced to come to know the fullness of God without us having to say a word. Our actions speak louder than words. Our body language says a lot about us. Esther quickly learned that in order to go before a king she had to be totally ready, physically and emotionally. She had to speak to the king in a certain royal language, and dress, walk and act confidently.

How do we speak to the king in our lives? After all, they are the priest and Lord of our homes. God put them in charge and I have realized after lots of battles that they will eventually get the respect they deserve.

How do we treat our children? Children follow a pattern after their parents. Every child says when growing up that they will not be like their parents. They then grow up doing the same things their parents did! It's amazing what the power of influence can do. A parent who smokes and drinks or curses will raise children to do the same thing. A parent, who serves the Lord, feeds the poor and takes in the homeless will raise kids to do the same also.

Pepe used to play rock music and wanted to open a rock band in his teenage years. Thank God he got saved before he could carry out his dreams. Twenty years down the road, we have three kids who are musicians. Matthew plays the guitar; Joshua plays the drums and Leah plays keyboard, saxophone and now her favorite, the guitar. The boys now play in the church band and also have their own contemporary band with other friends from their school. I told Pepe that the kids all followed after his ways because of his Golgi apparatus and genes! Pepe's dream came to pass in the kids.

I am determined, as a woman of the kingdom, to influence positively or not at all. I must do something that will help women all around the world to discover God's great purpose in their lives and help them achieve it. Women have a much greater purpose in life than just living, breathing, eating and giving birth. There are many people out there looking for a mentor, a friend and a positive model to pattern after. Who better equipped to be there for them than women of the kingdom?

Chapter 16
Love and Intimacy

Sometime ago I asked my kids what they thought love was. Leah said that love is heart warming, kissing, dating, getting presents, and popular boys! Joshua said, when you like somebody you quit being mean to them. Matthew said, love is being accepted. Pepe said that love is unconditional and very naïve. Other adults describe love as uncontrollable, feeling dizzy, head spinning, butterflies in stomach and weak in the knees

Some songs describe love as: "Love Hurts", "I'm All Out of Love", "I'm Lost Without you", and my favorite, "Lost in love" and on and on the list goes. There are so many wonderful Christian songs that describe God's love: "Amazing Grace", "Oh How I Love Jesus", "Jesus, Lover of My Soul" and hundreds of other great songs we can sing over and over again.

When I think about love I think about God and his unending love for me. I think about people close to me like my dear husband Pepe whom I love so much. I think about our children Matthew, Joshua and Leah who fills my heart with joy. I think about my family, friends and extended church family. I think about all the people whom I am so fond of and have lots of affection for. That brings a smile to me. We live in a world where love is a very confusing word. People go to school, succeed in graduating with their degrees, get great jobs paying lots of money. They further go on to acquire great homes and vehicles, yet, for most of those people love is the only subject that they failed at. They end up in separation and divorce so soon after marriage. Some single people date many others and yet cannot find "Mr."

or "Miss" right. They go on television dating games or dating agencies, and yet it does not work out.

What was it in Esther, that she only had one night to go before the king and yet succeeded in winning his love and intimacy that very night? I believe that together with all the intense preparation she went through physically, spiritually and emotionally, Esther was focusing on the needs of the king. She knew he needed someone with more than just a pretty face. He had his choice among hundreds of young, beautiful virgins but none could provide the comfort he found in Esther. There was just something about Esther. She was truly a shining star whose light shone far more than the others.

I believe that King Xerxes was looking for someone to replace his ex-wife Queen Vashti who would love him for who he was, and not for his riches and power. He needed someone who would reign with him in his empire and yet be respectful and submissive, someone to be there in his ups and downs and not think about their own comforts. Despite all the negative stories Esther heard about King Xerxes, she made up in her mind that he needs help and that she was not going in to judge him from the past. She began studying Song of Songs and she was going to give him all the love she could give. She remembered Proverbs 10:12 love covers over all wrongs.

And so, Esther spent the whole time of preparation researching the king's likes and dislikes. While the other virgins dressed to impress with the best robes and gowns, loaded with jewelry on every inch of their bodies, Esther went with a different approach. She was unique, simple yet elegant. She remembered that clothes alone do not make a person, and that she should render her heart and not her garments. What the king really wanted all along was a heart that loved and cared for him, someone who could tame his wildest impulses.

I think about people today who have problems such as drinking, smoking, abusive traits, who are in need of a friend who will come into their lives and help them turn their lives around, patiently and lovingly showing them how to live out their purpose.

People will not change by manipulation or force, so we can forget about this approach if this is indeed what some of us are trying to use to bring change. Call on God's name and see how fast He will bring positive changes to you and your loved ones without force.

By training her mind to look at the king positively, Esther prepared herself to be a lover and a friend to him. She decided to put the situation in God's hands, and trust him that he will work things out in her favor. She knew that God will be with her that night to see her through. So, by the time she approached the king's chambers, Esther remembered the story of Adam and Eve, how God made Eve for Adam by using one of Adam's own rib. We find this incredible true story in Genesis 2:22. Esther was about to become one flesh with King Xerxes, flesh of his flesh and bone of his bones. As the king stood in front of Esther she immediately remembered the following scripture;

How handsome you are my lover, oh how charming.
Song of Songs 1:15

My lover is radiant and ruddy, outstanding among ten thousand. His head is purest gold; his hair is wavy and black as a raven. His eyes are like doves by the water streams washed in milk, mounted like jewels. His cheeks are like beds of spices yielding perfume. His lips are like lilies dripping with myrrh. His arms are rods of gold set with crystal lights. His body is like polished Ivory decorated with sapphires. His legs are pillars of marble set on bases of pure gold. His appearance is like Lebanon, choice as its Cedars. His mouth is sweetness himself, he is altogether lovely. This is my lover and friend O daughters of Jerusalem.
Song of Songs 5:10-16

This was her first, up close encounter with the king and she was very pleased.

The king also had some thoughts of his own about Esther as she entered his chambers.

How beautiful you are my darling, your eyes are like doves, your hair is like a flock of goats descending from Mount Gilead, your teeth are like a flock of sheep just shorn, coming up from the washing, your lips are like a scarlet ribbon, your mouth is lovely. Your temples are like the halves of pomegranate. Your neck is like the tower of David, built with elegance. Your two breasts are like swans, like twin jaws of a gazelle. All beautiful you are my darling; there is no flaw in you.
Song of Songs 4:1-7

It was love at first sight. King Xerxes and Esther fell in love. They knew they were meant to be together from that very moment. They became intimate and they loved each other with such a great and pure love. This time it was different from all the other nights with all the other virgins. King Xerxes loved Esther more than all the others put together, and made her queen. He had no need to look any further, he found his rib. Esther had received the husband that she always prayed for, and would always love him and give him the love and respect he deserved.

I heard stories of married couples sleeping in separate rooms as the norm, and not being intimate for months or years. I wonder what could possibly be wrong. The Bible tells us that once we are married, our bodies do not belong to ourselves anymore, but to our spouses. We should not hold back love and intimacy from each other. It's against the Word of God according to 1 Corinthians 7:3-5. Theses couples have dated, courted and gotten to know each other, or so they thought, for years before marriage. Some have lived together for years as a trial basis before marriage only to have it fail in a short period of time. It goes to show that if God is not the foundation of any marriage and if He is not made a priority in their household, it will fail. It doesn't matter how much money or education is achieved.

I also believe that if underlying issues are not dealt with, like selfishness, sexual abuse, pornography, obesity, illness, sexual dysfunction, decreased desire for each other and infidelity, the marriage will definitely be in jeopardy. See your counselor, pastor or doctor for help if you have any of these problems. If you seek help, God will send it to you.

Pepe says that changing your mate will not solve the problem. If you leave your spouse for another, you may notice that you will still have marital problems. Seek help for yourself and your spouse before things get out of hand. Pray and read Gods word. He promised a great life if we seek him first;

> *Seek ye first the Kingdom of God and all his righteousness and all these things will be added onto you (a good marriage, children, health and everything you desire).*
>
> *Matthew 6:33*

As women of the kingdom, we need husbands who are great kings and lovers, and in this world we live in today, only God can grant us these kings. Study Song of Songs and prepare yourself for your husband to come to you, and when this ruddy, radiant man stand before you, you will know at once that he is the king you have been praying for. It would be love at first sight.

One night Pepe and I had a conversation with our kids in our bible study at home about love, sex, and marriage. The topic of sexually transmitted diseases and their prevention was brought up. After lengthy discussion, we came up with the solution that obeying the command of God about remaining virgins until marriage, was definitely the best and safest way to prevent those diseases like aids, hepatitis, syphilis, gonorrhea, or herpes. Purity is the only guarantee to a fulfilling and enjoyable life. All people need these days is a little self-control and things would be so much better in our world. Our love lives would be so intoxicating that there would be no room for separation and divorce. Isn't it great to be in love?

> *Many waters cannot quench love, rivers cannot wash it away!*
>
> *Song of Songs 8:7*

Chapter 17

A Worshiper

Who is a worshiper? It is one who pays homage, adoration, gives great regards, respect and honor to, someone who is honorable and distinguished and perfect. The only person I can think about who deserves such divine acts of honor is our great God, Jehovah, El Shadddai, Adonai, Emmanuel, Abba Father, Jesus Christ. He is the one who created the universe, plants, animals, and yes, human beings. How can we ignore Him totally like if He doesn't exist, or not acknowledge and be grateful for His great deeds?

Ascribe to the Lord the glory due to his name. Bring an offering, and come before him, worship the Lord in the splendor of his holiness. Give thanks to the Lord for he is good, his love endures forever.

1 Chronicles 16:29-34.

Have you ever noticed that before church services are held, even back in the days of the tabernacle that worshipers would go forth first? The Lord did command that Judah should go first, and Judah means praise and worship. That praise and worship is really warfare, breaking down strong holds that are present so that there will be no hindrances. Then, God could move in that specific place to do what He wants to do in the lives of people. This is done through Him releasing His glory upon us and teaching or healing through His word. He moves however and whenever He chooses to move, but Judah must go first.

I am reminded of the story of Joshua and the people of Jericho. The residents of Jericho had shut themselves behind stone walls for fear of the Israelites. What did the Israelites do? They built a stone monument to God, performed circumcision rituals and held a Passover celebration, this behavior unlike anyone has ever seen done, especially by an army. God sent a commander from His very own army to help Joshua and his army. God then told Joshua that He had delivered Jericho into his hands already, along with its king and fighting men. God further told Joshua to march around Jericho with all the armed men for six days. He instructed that seven priests should carry trumpets of ram's horns in front of the ark, and on the seventh day march around the city seven times with the priest blowing the trumpets. After the long blast of the trumpets all the people should give a loud shout, then the walls of the city will collapse. This true story is found in Joshua 6:2-5.

When Joshua and his people did as they were told and worshiped God with the trumpets and in the obedience of walking around the city so many times and shouting, the walls came down!

Shout, for the Lord has given you the city, was Joshua's command.

Joshua 6:15-17

Sometimes we need to shout in victory in anticipation of what God is about to do in our lives and see it come to pass. I think about Esther going before the king that day, un-summoned. What would have been her fate if she had not prayed and fasted for three days? I believe that things would have been very difficult. As children of God, we should not go before Him un-summoned. I believe that ways of going before Him un-summoned are when we are living in sin, holding on to anger, and envy, and bitterness, hatred towards our brothers or sisters. It would cause death to come upon us spiritually and our own petition would not be answered. It would be in vain.

The Bible tells us that God seeks worshipers, true worshipers who will worship Him in spirit and in truth.

John 4:23.

As women of the kingdom, how can we ever miss praise and worship on Sunday morning service? The most some people ever make it to church is on Sunday mornings, and if you are late for that too, what do you really get to keep you for the rest of the week until, maybe the next Sunday? And that is if you make it to church at all. Many people want God's blessing in their lives but are not ready and willing to pay a sacrifice for it. All God wants from us is our time and our worship. He wants to see if we are really interested in Him for who He is and not what He can do for us.

There are many ways in worshiping God. I usually start off by repenting first as King David did, then I like to read the scriptures full of God's word and loving promise to us. Then I praise God for His magnificence of who He is followed by words of gratitude for what He has done for me. While I am doing all this I have worship music playing softly in the background. The last part of this is my petitions towards Him, and then I thank Him for answering prayers. I love worship because it's fulfilling and I just love to worship my creator. The bible tells us that when the praises go up, the blessings come down. I could only imagine the many blessings that overflow our praise and worship team as they worship and praise God Sunday after Sunday. They go into battle and break down so many strong holds so that we could enjoy the word of God as it comes forth. Praise and worship is so vital to me. It's where I trade in my sorrows, pain and shame for the joy of the Lord. It's impossible to live a life without worship.

When I get ready to conquer my household chores, I need worship and lots of it to get me through. I put on my music and worship while I work. When Leah hears the music she says "mom has her music on, she's getting ready to work." The truth is, worship helps me through each and every day. The king chose Esther because she was close to God. Although he did not know this, she had a certain aura about her. She looked like a Kingdom citizen. The king also chose Esther because he saw that she was interested in him and not in his riches or power. When you spend time with God, you will also look like a Kingdom citizen and people who see you will wonder what is it about her that is so beautiful? And, you can lovingly reply, "I am a daughter of a King!"

Chapter 18
A Woman of Favor

What is favor?

Favor is described as friendly or kind regard; good will; approval; liking, unfair partiality; favoritism, a kind, obliging, friendly, or generous act to do someone a favor.

Favored :

> Provided with advantages; talented, and specially privileged!
> Esther 2:17- *Now the king was attracted to Esther more than any of the other women, and she won his favor and approval more than any of the other virgins. So he set a royal crown on her head and made her queen instead of Vashti.*

When Esther was crowned queen of Persia, all the other contestants were wondering what was her secret? Why not me? Why was she made queen? What makes her better than me?

People in the church ask the similar question from time to time. We say and think who does God love most? Why do the prayers of certain people seem to be answered more than the prayers of others? Is there a secret formula or personal asset that puts them closer to God?

God tells us in the Bible that He does not show any favoritism, and that we should not play favorites either. James 2:1 tells us and that if we play favorites, we sin. Yet, the way God treat each of us sometimes, we think we are His favorite, but, that's the way He spoils us. I do not believe that God plays favorites, but He does give favor to His children, each according to their level of desire and intimacy with Him. If someone worships more than the other, God has no choice but to show up in that worshiper's life and fill them up to capacity and overflowing. The same way, if one shows no interest in worship, why would God come and fill them up? He will be going against their will, forcing himself on them, and that would be favoritism. We would all agree that's unfair.

What did Esther do to gain such favor with God, king Xerxes and everyone around her in the palace? God was her main priority. Before Esther was chosen as queen, she went to Hegai, the king's chamberlain and eunuch and found out what style and color dress would the king like to see her wear, what perfume scents would he like to smell, and the protocol of proper approach to the king.

About protocol in approaching the king: When I wanted to meet the President of Guyana who was on the same flight out of Guyana as us, I could not just walk into first class and talk with him. I went to his body guard/ security personnel and asked him if I could meet the President and then he arranged the meeting. The president's Hegai was his body guard. Upon entering the room where he was we could not approach him hastily in any impolite or unethical way. The body guard said "here is his Excellency". As we went in I extended my hand to him and said "hello Your Excellency", just like his Hegai said it.

We all have ministry to God, but who will we allow to teach us to please Him in our service? The bible says He has given apostles, prophets, evangelists, pastors and teachers to prepare us for our ministry. Are we willing and obedient to be taught how to do ministry properly and please God?

There are chamberlains in these times here at the church waiting to help you become presentable before the king. Be teachable and draw form those chamberlains who have been in the king's chambers before. The pastor, elders, and some of the leaders are here to help you along the way. They will teach you how to move the heart of God.

Holiness is another way of living that would help us to get on the path towards favor.

We must have a pure heart. Matthew 5: Blessed are the pure in heart, for they will see God. We need to examine our heart daily, repent and ask forgiveness from God and those that we offend, denounce the things that we do wrong and strive to never do them again.

Our lifestyle has to change as kingdom citizens. We have to be different from the world.

We will have to stop going to certain places, speaking, acting, and dressing modestly. Lustful, worldly pleasures and immoral friends must be given up. Do not worry about losing friends. God will send you the friends you need.

The world should see a difference in us. The salt and light that we are need to show at all times.

When you walk in God's will, and give Him the time that's due to Him, prayer, praise and worship, God will cause you to become a woman of favor, He will stamp His seal of approval on you and you will receive more than you ever planted, and even where you have not planted. Blessings will come to you from every direction. You will not even have to look for them. People will just look at you and want to bless you.

I did not know a lot about favor, until I read the book by Tommy Tenney, "Finding Favor with the King." It opened up my eyes to a whole new world. I saw that I was missing out on so much because of my lack of knowledge in the area of favor. Ever since I read that book, my life has changed forever. It coincidently happened (of course nothing happened by coincidence!) as I was reading this book, I was informed about the Esther weekend that was about to take place in Dallas, Texas, TBN Studios, in November 2004. My first reaction was, "I have to go, I must be there, they cannot have an Esther weekend without me!"

My petition (legal demand) and good reason for this

statement was that I have been having Arise Esther Women Conferences at our church since 2000. If I were to be closest to anyone in the bible, it would be Esther. It was prophesied soon after my salvation in 1984 that my life would be like Esther's. Esther has been my role model ever since. The name of our women's group at church is "The Esther Gathering." I had too many good reasons why I must be at the Esther weekend! I would have an experience that would complete my heart desires. And so, I started the mission to see how I could get there. I called productions and they informed me that they were all booked. I had to resort to plan B, ask my spiritual mother and friend Pastor Ruth Munroe if she would take me with her. She was out of town so I had to wait twenty four hours, the longest twenty four hours of my life, to get a reply!

Have you ever prayed non-stop for twenty four hours? Well I did! I prayed, petitioned, praised, and reminded God of the fact that he told me that I am an Esther. I showed him the face (the irresistible face Tommy Tenney talks about in his book). When I called the next day to find out the answer, I was overwhelmed with joy. Pastor Ruth said that she had someone else in mind for that one open spot, but she would take me instead! Is that favor or what? I had won great favor with God and man. I thank God for Pastor Ruth, a wonderful woman of God.

I could not wait for the next three months to come. With the help of the beautiful women at MCCI, I tried to lose a few pounds and did, they took me to the spa, had my hair done etc. and I was ready to go. It was a most wonderful experience. We were pampered by the Godchasers leaders and interns, ministered to and got an opportunity of a life time in being extras in the movie, "One Night with the King." My life has never been the same since, thank God for the Godchasers Network. I have been walking in the favor of the Lord and it's unbelievable to see all the doors God has now opened in my life. To have favor with God and man is one of the greatest miracles to ever achieve. If

Esther, I and many other God fearing people can receive favor, I want to tell you that since God plays no favorites, he can open up a door of favor for you also. It's not difficult to do, rather its enjoyable seeking the Lord so much and spending lots of time with Him. I have many, many stories of favor; you would think I am bragging. But, I will be bragging on God, boasting on His love and goodness towards me. God tells us to boast on Him.

Let not the wise man boast of his wisdom or the strong man boast of his strength or the rich man boast of his riches, but let him who boasts, boast about this, that he understands and knows me, that I am the Lord, who exercise kindness, justice and righteousness on earth, for in these I delight.
Jeremiah 9:23

If you have a confident living relationship with God, its worth boasting about because this is what counts. God prefers to take the weak and poor, those who have little to boast about, and make them into somebody.

Esther came into the palace weak and poor, as many of us come into this world weak and poor, with no worldly inheritance. As we submit to God and show that we are interested in Him, He will in turn make us women of favor, favor that has been there in the kingdom all along waiting for us. When favor comes to us because we have remained holy and worshiped Him always, it doesn't matter who is in line in front of us. They are bypassed and the blessing comes to us.

Remember queen Vashti who was before Esther? God caused her to be demoted and removed to make place for Esther, and He will do the same for you in your jobs and everywhere else that you need it.

Start seeking our God and king now, and see what is waiting ahead for us. It's an abundance of favor!

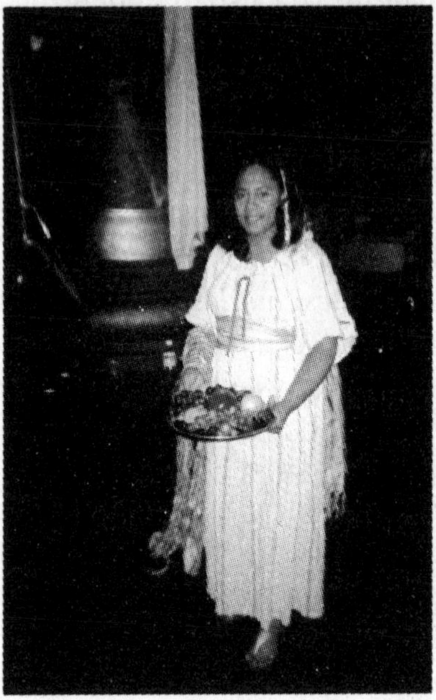

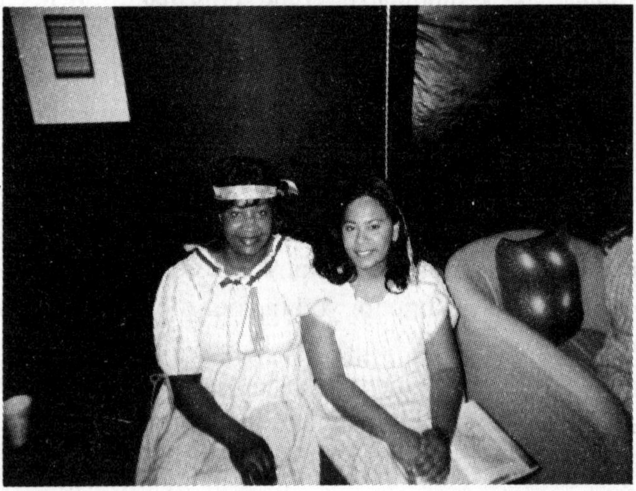

Chapter 19

A Warrior

It was still during the honeymoon period that trouble came into Esther's life once again. Haman, the king's right hand man decided that it's time for the Jews to be totally wiped out from the Persian Empire once and for all. This was an old issue that was never solved between the Amalekites and the Jews even before Esther was born. This massacre was to take place on the 13th day of the 12th month. Haman somehow succeeded on getting the king's blessing on this evil plan. He was very sly and convincing.

This situation was placed in Esther's hands by her cousin Mordecai. He thought that God had put Esther in the palace for such a time as this. This story is found in *Esther 4:14*. Esther was not only in trouble in her marriage (the king did not know she was a Jew), but now there were external problems. She had the burden of coming up with a plan to save her people. She had no friends to call upon, no counselors available to tell her what to do. She told herself, "I knew it. It was too good to be true, nothing comes easy for me. There's a price to pay, of course, nobody but Esther to the rescue." Again Esther did not see any sense in arguing with God that He should use someone else. She was used to these surprises by now. She stopped feeling alone as she remembered the scripture;

I will never leave you nor forsake you. I will be with you to the end.
             Isaiah 41:10

Esther felt a great compassion come over her. With only

a few days left to come up with a solution, Esther had to get to work and work fast. She had not seen the king in a month. He was probably busy planning another one of his missions to conquer some neighboring province for his empire.

Is the enemy closing in on you?

Do you have a time sensitive issue that will determine your destiny?

Well, Esther and all the other Jews had one too, the 13th day of Adar.

What would they do? Esther quickly responded. It's time for warfare! I am a woman of passion and authority, I am going to fight this and change the king's mind without saying a word. She told Mordecai to get the message out to all the Jews that they would fight this one on their knees. Esther knew that these things come only through prayer and fasting, so she declared, no food or drink for three days.

Want to get rid of some Hamans in your life? Try fasting and praying for a while and you would see great results.

Esther had to fast in secret, the king could not notice. Only the Jews and her royal maids knew and fasted with her. She could not wear sackcloth and ashes. She had to wear regular clothes, makeup as usual so no one in the palace would know that she was fasting. She said, "When the fast is over, I would go before the king and risk my life. Although it is against the law to go before the king un-summoned I will go, and if I perish, I perish!" Meanwhile, Haman was building the gallows to hang Mordecai.

What do you do when you have pressing situations coming your way?

Whenever I have a situation that I need help with, I always call upon some of my confidants, and the intercessors. I ask them to pray and agree with me for victory in those areas. Never try to do warfare alone. Scriptures tells us that one can put a thousand, but two can put ten thousand to flight. Imagine Esther and the whole Jewish nation praying. Could you imagine all the tens of thousands of demons that were chased out of Susa and the entire Persian Empire within those three days?

On the third day Esther got up from her prostrate position, stood up straight with a confidence that could have only come from God and said, "No king has ever, or will ever intimidate God no matter how powerful or wealthy they are." Esther now knew that God could change anyone. She remembered the scripture : Stand still and see the salvation of the Lord.

Exodus 14:13-14

Esther was going to go before the king, un-summoned. She was ready, even if she had to face death, to take a risk that very few people would want to take. She was convinced that God was about to do something spectacular. She took a bath in mineral salts, put on the king's favorite dress, the red one that hugs her body so well, she put on his favorite perfume, her best high heel shoes, her makeup, and best jewelry.

She looked at herself in the mirror and finally topped it all off with her gold and diamond crown, smiled confidently, strode across the royal courts and into the king's chambers. Suddenly she had no fear, no shaking, and no cold or sweaty hands. She was upright and confident that God was with her. She had done her part praying and fasting. Now it was up to God to do the rest. As the king was speaking to his men about their new ambush plans, he smelled this wonderful, familiar fragrance, the one he liked to smell, and only one person wears this fragrance, Esther. Esther is nearby, could it really be her?

He lost his train of thought, looked up and had to blink his eyes a few times. Esther was radiating with the glory of God, just glowing from God's presence. The king looked at her red lips, darkened eyelids and long eyelashes, rosy cheeks, beautiful dark hair, her body draped in fine red linen. His eyes twinkled, his mouth opened, his jaw dropped and he was now drooling. King Xerxes held out the scepter before he could even think whether he should hold it out or not. He had just broken his own rule that anyone approaching the king un-summoned by him should be put to death. All he knew was that Esther, the Queen of Persia was standing before him, and she was beautiful, and all his. Esther touched the scepter and connected with the king *Esther 5:3*. The king then asked Esther what was her request, that up to half the kingdom would be hers! If you seek the king in fasting and prayer you will not even have to ask God for anything. He will be asking you what you want, and all your hearts desire would be granted. Esther was a person of patience and discernment; she realized that it was not the time or place to tell the king about Haman's wicked plots. She invited him and Haman to a banquet. Later on at the banquet the king again asked Esther what was her request and again offered her half of the kingdom. Esther realized that he was not ready to hear it, and invited them to another banquet the next day. The king was happy to honor Esther's request.

Not only was the way being made straight for Esther, but Mordecai was also in for a treat. On the night of the first banquet, the king could not sleep, so he had his chamberlains read him the book of Chronicles where he was reminded of a man who saved his life from an assassination attempt. The man's name happened to be Mordecai! The king then asked if anything was done to reward this Mordecai. They informed him that nothing was done. The next morning King Xerxes asked Haman to officially honor and dignify this man who saved his life. Haman thought it was himself, but he soon found out that it was Mordecai. As outraged as Haman was he had to obey the king and carry out this extensive honoring of Mordecai, the man he hated most! Haman thought he was dreaming and having a nightmare. He could not raise his head in public and went home with his face covered in shame. When you think that no one sees the great sacrifices you do for the kingdom, God sees and will never let it go unrewarded.

I delight greatly in the Lord, my soul rejoices in my God. For the lord has clothed me with garments of salvation, and carried me in a robe of righteousness.

Isaiah 61:10

The next day came and it was time for the second banquet. The king again asked Esther what her request was and again offered her up to half of the kingdom. Esther knew it was time to tell the king her concerns. She proceeded to tell the king the secret that she kept from him about her identity and about Haman's wicked plot against herself and her people. The king, who loved Esther so much, became so outraged that he immediately sentenced Haman to death without asking him any questions. Of course Haman was begging Esther to have mercy on him but it was too late, it was out of Esther's hands and in the king's hands now, a much higher authority. Haman and his sons were all executed in the same gallows that they had built for Mordecai. God does not like to see his children persecuted by anyone and he eventually puts an end to them. The enemy can only go so far and then God steps in and says, "That's enough, be gone Satan." The king then allowed the Jews to defend themselves on the 13th day of Adar, which they did very well because God was with them.

Esther 18:17 tells us that many people of all different nationalities became Jews at that time because fear of the Jews had seized them! Why did all this deliverance come? Because one person, Esther, thought that she could make a difference. By fasting and praying she believed that the heart of her king could be changed and that the enemy would be destroyed forever. And so he was.

If we were to refer back to an event in our lives in which we know that it was God and only Him who brought us through it, what would it be?

I remember my near death experience that resulted from

a prophecy I had received when I was only twelve years old. My parents had officially christened me into the religion that they were a part of at that time. On that day, when the prayer was over, the priest read the palms of my hands and told me he saw my death in the future. He said that I would die at nineteen years old, and if I did not die then, I would die at thirty years old of a terrible disease. Why would a fully grown man of any religion tell a child this? I thought I was doomed for death. I thank God that as Pepe and I were dating, he got saved and later on lead me to the Lord. I was saved at 19 years old!

A few months after I got saved I went on a hiking expedition with the church into the deep jungles of Trinidad that led us to a beautiful, big, waterfall called Paria Falls. Our pastors warned us not to go too far into the lake because it was deep. Of course I tried to swim across to the other side where they were, got tired in the middle, and thought I would stand up and rest a while. Instead, I started going down, down, and down. I could not touch ground for a while. I thought, "That's it, I'm dead." I became tired and stopped fighting and let go emotionally and physically. As I did that, my feet touched ground and I did not know where I got the strength to kick up and reach the surface again, and swim back out to the waters edge! God had saved my life, and I knew that if I did not come to know the true God just a few months before this day, I would have died just like the prophecy said.

All went well until I turned thirty. The devil reminded me that I was going to die in that year. I had forgotten about the prophecy until he reminded me of it. Every day for 365 days I was tormented about death. I told no one about this, not even Pepe. I thought this was something I had to fight alone, with God's help.

I started getting physically sick. One day I started shaking in work. I was so cold that all the blankets and hot tea they gave me did not help me. The temperature that day was like 90 degrees. Pepe had to pick me up and take me home. I could not even drive because I was shivering too much. I started having chest pains, general malaise and terrible pains in my jaw and facial muscles whenever I ate my meals. I went to the doctor and explained all my symptoms. She did some tests and on my next visit, she said that my thyroid was way out of range. The level was up to 120 and the normal range is usually 6-10! She further told me that I would have to take thyroid medication for the rest of my life or else my body would shut down and I would die. I told her that I would not be taking any thyroid medication. I filled the prescription and brought it home and put it on the fireplace, but I never touched it. Then the Lord allowed me to attend a women's conference where they had a health session, and the speaker mentioned thyroid problems and herbal supplements for them.

I went and got the herbal supplements and started taking them. I pitched the prescription thyroid medication into the garbage, it was never opened. (Please do not try this at home. Each person should know your own level of faith and work it accordingly). After a few months, I went back to the doctor for my check up and my thyroid level was down to normal and has been that way every time I check it. That year of my 30th year period was the most difficult. I prayed like I never prayed before in my life. I found all the scriptures that conquered death and sickness and repeated them daily. The night before my 31st birthday, I remained awake until it was midnight. I had now turned 31 and I was still alive! The battle was over. If I had to do it over again I would tell Pepe and the intercessors so that the battle could have been much easier.

From then on, I do not battle anything on my own. There are people out there who care, and are ready and willing to fight with us. Nevertheless the battle is God's, not ours. We fight on our knees.

When problems come our way how do we handle it?

Is it time to get depressed and hold a pity party?

I have learned that focusing on the problem will not solve anything. It doesn't matter what the problem is or how serious it is, with God all things are possible. Through all my life's trials I have noticed that it was warfare that saved me every time.

Warfare doesn't always have to be loud and aggressive. Sometimes it can be, but other times it can be praying and crying out to God. Warfare is also knowing and quoting the scriptures.

Pepe and I fasted for our middle son Joshua one day. He is always being attacked by the enemy. Last August the devil tried to kill all our 3 children in a car accident. Josh was driving. The car was totaled, but thank God no bones were broken. As we were fasting and praying for him, he was being tormented that night and could not sleep. Demons were telling him all night that he is going to kill him, and his friends.

At 5.30 in the morning, I felt an acute sinus attack and I got out of bed and started to go downstairs for my medicine. Josh said mom is that you? I said yes and started going towards his room. He told me what he was battling all night so I woke Pepe up from sleep and went downstairs.

As Pepe went in his room Josh told him; "Mom is powerful, from the moment she started coming towards my room, the demons started running out. They were afraid of Mom"!

Prayer and fasting does wonders and it makes demons afraid of us! When we know the scriptures, those promises that God has for us, that we shall live and not die, that we are bought with a price, we are lenders and not borrowers, more than conquerors, the head and not the tail, over comers, covered by the blood, Holy Ghost filled, highly favored, what can keep us down?

Pepe and I have learned to live a lifestyle of fasting and praying, and because of this we have seen many breakthroughs.

What is your dilemma today?

If the king is for you who can be against you?

If the king loves you, does it matter who hates you?

Haven't you seen the enemy collapse before your very eyes every time?

Didn't you know that those who disgrace you and spit on you will need you again one day?

What is your petition? The king wants to know today. And the same deliverance God brought to Esther, He will bring to you.

Chapter 20

A Woman of Celebration

After having such a difficult life growing up as an orphan, becoming captive at the palace, then having to face the king that appointed night, Esther's long suffering paid off. The king loved Esther and made her queen. Her life became a life of celebration and continues up to this day during Purim. When the king decided that Esther was the one to become his queen, he set the royal crown on her head and made her queen, replacing Queen Vashti. Then, he gave a great banquet known as Esther's banquet for all his nobles and officials. He proclaimed a holiday throughout the provinces and distributed gifts with royal liberality. This true story is found in *Esther 2:17-18*.

There was further celebration when deliverance came to the Jews on the 14 and 15th day of Adar. They had defended themselves so well and had gathered so many spoils, that they did not have room enough to hold it. The battle was extended for another day giving the Jews more opportunity to defeat and conquer the enemy! Mordecai was given the king's signature ring that was removed from Haman, which made him governor of Persia and second in command to the King Xerxes. Esther was given Haman's house, which she in turn gave to Mordecai.

After the battles were over, the rejoicing started. They had a day of feasting and gladness. Another public holiday was declared (Purim) and is still celebrated by the Jews up to this day. This celebration includes gladness and feasting, sending presents to one another, mocking Haman by

wearing masks, feeding and giving gifts to the poor.
Esther 9:22.

We make it a custom in our family to show thankfulness and gratefulness to God by celebrating every birthday and anniversary that he allows us to see. Everyone gets a party and celebration on these occasions. I remember when our eldest son Matthew got his driver's license, the whole family was there, including his grandparents! We watched, and prayed as he drove off with the licensing officer. We were on the edge until the test was over. He got out of the car and signaled thumbs up as he rushed off, following the officer to have his picture taken, and pay the fees. We celebrated by going out to dinner that evening. This was one of the happiest days of our lives. We would have one less kid to pick up and drop off, and their schedules were busier than ours!

Little did Pepe know that he would eventually lose his car to Matthew, the next day! We woke up the next morning and heard a car pulling out of the driveway; we rushed to look out the window. It was Matthew driving off to school! He never got on the school bus again! We did not know that he was so brave to drive to school all by himself, but thank God he was. Our second son Joshua was also happy and celebrating. He announced, "Thank God Matt got his license, now he can take me wherever I need to go." Joshua has a lot of friends, as he is the people person in the family. He always has many, many places to visit!

Another celebration is when our kids do well on their report cards. They are rewarded with money depending on how many A's and B's they receive. This is one good reason we motivate our kids into showing us their report cards!

Pepe and I have started an awards program at the church. It is sponsored by our own company Dove Environmental Labs. Every year, in June we have the Dove Environmental scholastic awards for all the graduating students and students receiving the honor roll. All the kids make sure their parents bring in those certificates on time so that they could be recognized and celebrated. The parents report that their kids are so happy that they go home boasting and proud, and display their trophies and medallions for everyone to see.

When I turned 40, the women at the church gave me a big celebration party to help me cross into middle age gracefully! They surprised me with a dinner cruise, and many wonderful gifts. I will forever be grateful to them for their love and help in this stage of life. I have always believed that the forties should be the prime of our lives. It should be a time when we enjoy the fruit of our labor, the wine from our vineyards and the cream of our crops. I thank God that these expectations were met, far beyond my imagination. It feels great to be in my forties. For all of you women approaching mid life, come on over celebrating! It feels great!

Another celebration is for our wedding anniversaries. Each year we go to different countries to spend our anniversary. Pepe loves it, and is thrilled about getting his passport stamped with lots of stamps for different countries around the world! However, he doesn't like to go on very long airplane rides. 3 to 4 hours is his tolerance level. Since our next anniversary is going to be our 20th year, I told Pepe we have to go far away, either Hawaii or England. He did his calculation and saw that it would take fewer hours to fly to England than Hawaii, so he chose England! I am happy and celebrating either way.

I believe that another way of celebrating is by giving God thanks and praise through testimonies of what he has done for us.

Give thanks unto the Lord, call upon his name, and make known among the nation what he has done.
1 Chronicles 16:8

When I think about this scripture I think about Christmas, celebrating Jesus' birth by exchanging presents with friends and family. I think about Easter sunrise service, rising early in the morning to give God thanks and recognition for dying on the cross, then coming back to life again. I think about Thanksgiving

Day in America. A day set aside just to be thankful and acknowledge the great union and cooperation between the Native American Indians and the Pilgrims who left Europe to escape religious persecution at that time. These Pilgrims risked it all for the glory of God, and, because of that risk, helped America to become this wonderful and great nation it is today.

Revelation 12:11 tells us that *we overcome Satan by the blood of the lamb and the word of our testimony.*

When we celebrate, the enemy is fully put to shame. Haman and the Amalekites were surely put to shame, destroyed, never to hurt Esther and the Jews again. Esther the orphan became a queen over an entire Empire.

What battles are you going through at this time?

Does it seem like it's extended for a longer time?

Just remember the longer the battle the larger the spoils. *Psalm 30:5* says that *weeping may endure for a night, but joy comes in the morning.*

Start preparing your victory party, a grand celebration, while the Lord is fighting your battles for you. Although the king found out that Esther was a Jew and she hid it from him, it did not matter because he loved her. If God did this for Esther, he can surely do it for you.

Isaiah 61:7-9 says *instead of their shame, my people will receive a double portion, and instead of disgrace they will rejoice in their inheritance, and so they will inherit a double portion in their land, and everlasting joy will be theirs.*

For I the Lord love justice; I hate robbery and iniquity. In my faithfulness I will reward them and make an everlasting covenant with them. Their descendants will be known among the nations and their offspring among the peoples. All who see them will acknowledge that they are a people the Lord has blessed!

God is a God who keeps his promises, and he promised

us an entire Kingdom, filled with Righteousness, Peace and Joy in the Holy Ghost. Do not settle for a quarter or half of the Kingdom, but the entire Kingdom like Esther did. The time has come for women of the Kingdom to walk in prosperity, health, peace and unending favor.

Let the celebration begin!

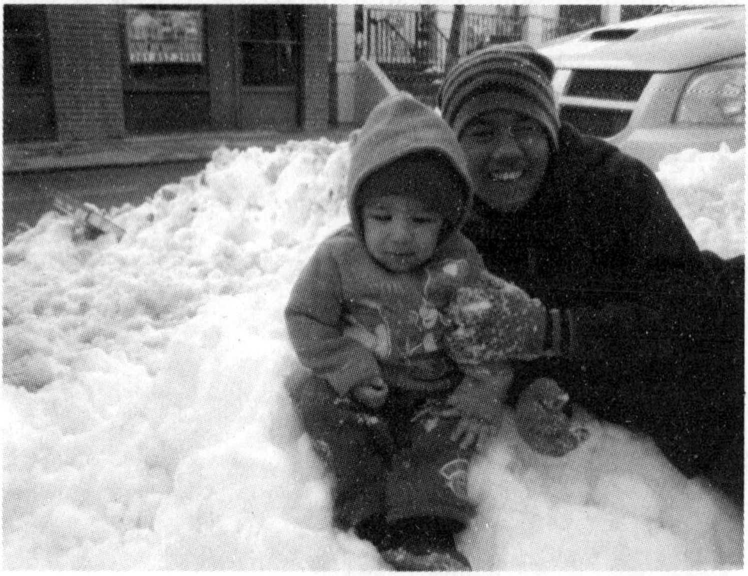

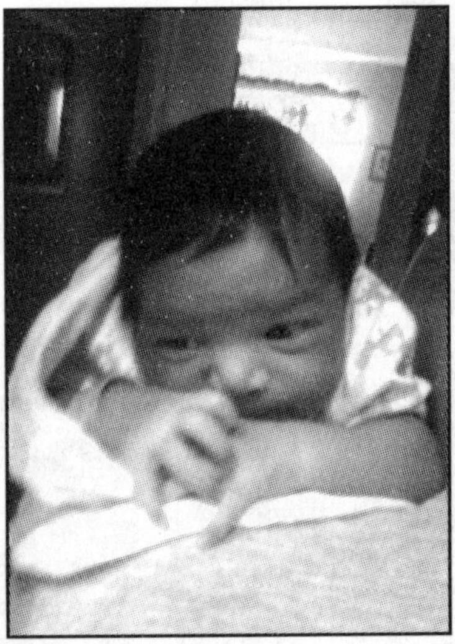

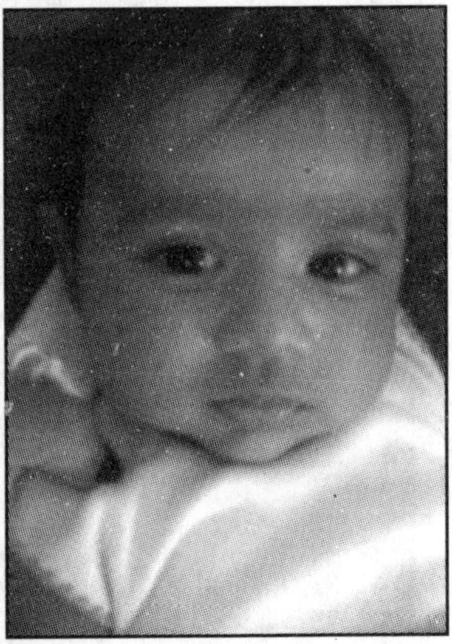

Esther Gathering Information

The Esther Gathering Women's Conferences are held every year either at Miramar Christian Center International in Miramar Florida or in different countries around the world.

Also, for any individual Woman or Women groups around the world who are interested in networking with, and becoming part of the Esther Gathering, please contact us for further information. This is a great opportunity of getting women from all different parts of the world to come together in the kingdom of God to fulfill our great purpose.

Please feel free to contact us.
Write to:
The Esther Gathering
Miramar Christian Center International
7984 Miramar Parkway
Miramar, Florida 33023
Phone: 954-989-7300
Email address: esthergathering@mccint.org or
mcc@mccint.org
Website – www.mccint.org

About The Author

*A*ngela Ramnath PhD is the wife of Dr. Pepe Ramnath, Senior Pastor of Miramar Christian Center International. They have been married since 1986, and have three beautiful children, Matthew, Joshua, and Leah. She was born in the island of Trinidad & Tobago to Siew & Sarah Radhay and has three siblings.

Angela is a registered nurse by profession. She received her RN degree at the School of Nursing, General Hospital San Fernando Trinidad, and is also certified in the states of Florida and Indiana. Angela studied marriage and relational counseling studies with Light University in an association with the American Association of Christian Counselors. She recently received an Honorary Doctor's degree with specialization in Counseling from the Academy of Universal Global Peace in Chennai India. Angela is presently the Vice President of Dove Environmental Laboratories where she works at this time. She is the author of Arise Esther, Becoming Women of the Kingdom and is working on publishing two other books at this time. Besides working at Dove Labs and taking care of the home and children, Angela finds time in her busy schedule to help her husband in ministry and administrate the Esther Gathering Women's Ministry and Conferences both nationally and internationally. These conferences are attended by thousands.

God has called Angela to ministry, in the area of family, marriage, and mentoring women. She believes that ministry should be fun, enjoyable, adventurous and tangible or else it should not be done.

Part of Angela's extensive adventures includes being an extra in the movie by Tommy Tenney, "One Night with the King." Her illustrated sermons add humor and practical insights for effective Kingdom living.

Bibliography

In Pursuit of Purpose - Dr Myles Munroe
Finding Favor with the King - Tommy Tenney
No Greater Love - Mother Teresa
The Student Bible; NIV
Woman of Faith Study Bible; NIV

Other Publications of Bethlehem Publishers

(AKA Gospel For Every Tongue & Tribe)

ਰੂਹ ਦੀ ਖੁਰਾਕ
ਲੇਖਕ ਜਤਿੰਦਰ ਪ੍ਰਕਾਸ਼

ਸ਼ਤਾਨ ਦੀ ਫਾਹੀ
ਲੇਖਕ ਜਾੱਨ ਬਵੀਰ

ਇੱਕ ਲੜਕੀ ਕੇ ਸਮਾਨ ਲੜੇ
ਲੇਖਕ ਲੀਸਾ ਬਵੀਰ

BETHLEHEM PUBLISHERS COMMITTED IN :
Translating
Publishing
Printing
Distribution of Christian books and literature.

सफलता के सत सिधांत-(Hindi) DVDs
The Power of the Spoken Word (Hindi & English) DVDs
Buried with Christ(Baptism)-मसीह के साथ दफन-(Hindi) DVDs

Phone USA: 718-785-5921
          INDIA: 98881-90529

Email us:
info@BethlehemPunjabiChurch.com
Log on to:
www.RuhdiKhurak.com
www.BethlehemPublishers.co.cc